Breakfast
All Day

Breakfast
All Day

◆

150 Recipes
for Everybody's
Favorite Meal

◆

Edon Waycott

Hearst Books
New York

Library of Congress Cataloging-in-Publication Data

Waycott, Edon.
Breakfast all day : 150 recipes for everybody's favorite meal / by Edon Waycott.
p.   cm.
ISBN 0–688–13133–6
Includes index.
1. Breakfasts.   I. Title.
TX733.W39   1996
641.5'2—dc 20   95-48880
CIP

Printed in the United States of America

First Edition

1 2 3 4 5 6 7 8 9 10

BOOK DESIGN BY BEVERLEY PERKIN

To my children, Bradford and Jennifer,
who tested my creativity as well as my patience at breakfast,
but who I wish were still at my table

Acknowledgments

The idea for this book had been rumbling around in my head for a long time, but my hard-working agents, Maureen and Eric Lasher, deserve thanks for making it all happen. ✳ Thanks to everyone who shared their breakfast routines with me: Jeff Wells, my personal trainer, whose bright mind and inspiring teaching are great motivations; Rod and Mona Spector, two of the fittest people I know; my dear friend, Maida Hastings, whose intellect, discipline, and eating habits are treasured attributes of our friendship. ✳ Thanks to Alice and Alan Cunningham of Malibu Fig Tree Ranch whose passion for growing the most wonderful figs is contagious. My continued appreciation to Mark Peel and Nancy Silverton for allowing my jams to accompany their outstanding breakfasts at Campanile. ✳ A special thanks to editor Kathleen Hackett whose sunny voice, sharp mind, and sparkling vision encouraged me at every juncture of this book. A real joy to work with! Thanks to Dana Gallagher for her fine photography. And always, warm thanks and gratitude to my devoted husband, Ralph, who brings fresh squeezed juice to me in bed every morning and never complains about the chaos I leave in the kitchen.

Contents

◆

Breakfast
All Day

Introduction

I grew up in a family that took breakfast very seriously. My great-grandmother ate a sweet potato with fried oysters every morning of her adult life, and she lived to be eighty-three. My father's ritual of combining several dry cereals with half of a precisely cut banana continues to this day. My sister and I were never allowed to leave for school without consuming at the very least an egg, a piece of toast, and a glass of juice. On weekends we ate late breakfasts that consisted of pancakes with warm maple syrup, coffee cakes that filled the house with a sweet bakery-fresh aroma, or egg-and-milk saturated French toast accompanied by homemade sausage. Sometimes we had breakfast for Sunday night supper: omelets, Welsh rarebit with sautéed tomatoes, fried egg sandwiches, or whole-wheat crêpes with warm, just-made applesauce. When we were sick, my mother would bring us cozy bowls of cream of wheat cereal topped with a sprinkling of brown sugar and two oven-toasted pieces of very thinly sliced bread with no butter. This comfort food was served on a wooden bed tray with a side pocket for magazines. In our house breakfast—whether eaten morning, noon, or night—was a favorite meal. It's no wonder I love eating breakfast all day. ✳ The rite of eating breakfast was something I tried to pass on to my own children. A hyperactive son and a daughter who was a picky eater made early schoolday mornings a balancing act for me as I tried to prepare nutritious breakfasts they would eat while packing school lunches. Early on I discovered that familiar, wholesome foods packaged in different forms could spark the interest of my children in the morning and send them off with smiles instead of scowls. A scrambled egg sandwiched inside a toasted English muffin was easier to handle; a "good morning" pizza of ricotta and sliced peaches drizzled with apricot preserves had instant appeal; fruit, yogurt, protein powder, and a little molasses blended into a milk shake was easier to swallow on a morning when an oral report was due. I made a toasted oat cereal that had the familiar taste of an oatmeal cookie but far less sugar and no fat. I baked banana bran muffins from a batter stirred together the night before and tucked one into the lunch bag in place of store-bought cookies to ensure extra energy for the afternoon. ✳ Eating a good breakfast, no matter what your age, provides long-lasting vitality and keeps the mind alert and stamina high. A great first meal of the day gives the body fuel to burn and brings the mind into sharper focus after the night's rest. During the five years I was a single parent, I made extra efforts to start mornings with my kids on a positive note. ✳ Quiches, omelets, frittatas, and other egg dishes know no hour, appearing on brunch menus, lunch menus, and light-supper-before-the-theater menus. Scones, muffins, quick breads, jams, and compotes of fruits are served at tea as well as breakfast. On the other hand, foods thought to have a place only at lunch or dinner can be served at breakfast. French toast sandwiches with ham, grilled figs and prosciutto, burritos filled with scrambled eggs and salsa, and potato-crusted tomato and gorgonzola pie are welcome interpretations of regular breakfast offerings. ✳ Many people will tell you that they like breakfast, just not the first thing in the morning. If your family is among them, try to redefine traditional breakfast foods to include dishes previously thought of as un-breakfast items. Serve a baked potato topped with yogurt and goat cheese or a frozen yogurt milk shake. Since nearly everyone has a blender and so little time on weekday mornings, breakfast-in-a-glass can be whirred up in a flash for kids and adults who live in the morning fast lane. ✳ *Breakfast All Day* provides innovative ways to think about and put together a balanced breakfast with foods drawn from all meals. Breakfast can be *anything* you would eat at any other time of day. And, conversely, breakfast food can become your lunch or dinner food. Think lighter, fresher, simpler, and familiar, and indulge in your favorite tastes no matter what time of day it is. By redefining what breakfast can be, you will find it easier to expand the opportunity of having those favorite foods all day. Whether you prepare a salad for breakfast or eggs for dinner, a balanced, delicious meal can be assembled with the real tastes you crave. ✳ Breakfast is an intensely personal meal, defined by habits and tradition. In this book I want to show how it's also the one with the most variety of foods from which to choose. It's a beginning, another chance to try, a source of energy for the day. I think that's why the first meal of the day is so appealing to me; it's about adventure, a fresh start, taking control over something for yourself, or sending someone else off for the day with warmth and care. But it's also about repeating some of those foods that carry such positive associations throughout the other meals of the day. ✳ In this book I draw on my southern heritage of homemade goodness and nourishment from the heart and combine it with an attitude toward good nutrition and healthier ingredients.

Eggs

Eggs are instant problem solvers when there is nothing in the cupboard to provide a quick meal. A few fresh eggs, vegetables, and a sprinkling of cheese are all you need to make a frittata. And the beauty of a frittata is that it is just as satisfying for lunch or dinner as it is for breakfast. Eggs scrambled into leftover pasta can make the transition too. Eggs become portable meals when tucked into pita bread or tortillas or used as the filling for a bagel sandwich. Their creaminess when the yolks are soft balances the pungent vegetables of a pipérade. As you allow your imagination to expand the breakfast menu beyond morning, try to envision eggs in other meals throughout the day. ✳ Although eggs are reliably fresh when purchased from a supermarket, those that are newly laid have a taste that is hard to describe. If an egg is really fresh, the white and yolk cling together to form one unit when cracked open. The yolk's color ranges from pale yellow to deep orange, depending on what the chicken was fed. ✳ If you want or need to limit your intake of eggs, substitute 1 egg plus 1 egg white for every 2 eggs when scrambling or making omelets or use a commercial egg substitute.

Zucchini and Feta Frittata

Zucchini is available year round, so this recipe knows no season. If your late-summer garden is anything like mine, then you'll likely find yourself making this simple, tasty frittata more than once a week! It makes an ideal lunch or light supper and is perfect picnic food.

1 pound zucchini (4 to 5 small), thinly sliced

$^{1}/_{4}$ cup finely chopped onion

Salt

4 large eggs

1 teaspoon dried oregano or 2 teaspoons finely chopped fresh oregano

1 tablespoon finely chopped flat-leaf parsley

$^{1}/_{4}$ cup diced red bell pepper

$^{1}/_{4}$ teaspoon coarsely ground black pepper

2 tablespoons olive oil

$^{2}/_{3}$ cup crumbled feta cheese

Salsa and chopped fresh cilantro for serving

PLACE the zucchini and onion in a colander, sprinkle lightly with salt, and drain for $^{1}/_{2}$ hour. Rinse and blot dry with paper towels.

Place an oven rack 4 inches from the broiler unit and preheat the broiler.

Meanwhile, in a small bowl, whisk the eggs and set aside. In another small bowl, toss the zucchini and onion with the oregano, parsley, bell pepper, $^{1}/_{4}$ teaspoon salt, and black pepper. Heat the olive oil over high heat in a 10-inch ovenproof nonstick skillet. Add the zucchini mixture and cook until the slices are lightly browned. Quickly whisk the eggs again and pour onto the zucchini. Cook until the bottom of the frittata is golden brown and set around the edges.

Sprinkle the frittata with the cheese and place under the broiler. When the eggs are just set and the cheese is softened, remove the pan from the broiler. Loosen the bottom and sides of the frittata with a spatula and slide it out onto a serving plate, cheese side up. Serve with salsa and chopped cilantro.

Serves 4

Artichoke and Potato Frittata

Eggs and potatoes form a perfect partnership. And when artichokes are added to the mix, the results are superb. Serve this with steamed tender green beans or sugar snap peas for a light meal.

3 tablespoons olive oil

1 medium baking potato (about ½ pound), cut into ½-inch-thick wedges

One 13¼-ounce can artichoke hearts, quartered, drained, and rinsed

4 large eggs

2 cloves garlic, minced

2 teaspoons finely chopped fresh thyme or ½ teaspoon dried thyme

¼ teaspoon salt

¼ teaspoon coarsely ground black pepper

½ cup grated Parmesan cheese

2 tablespoons chopped flat-leaf parsley

PLACE an oven rack 4 inches from the broiler unit and preheat the broiler.

Meanwhile, in a 10-inch ovenproof nonstick skillet, heat 2 tablespoons of the olive oil over medium-high heat and sauté the potato and artichoke hearts until lightly browned on all sides. Remove the pan from the heat and transfer the mixture to a plate using a slotted spoon. In a medium bowl, whisk together the eggs, garlic, thyme, salt, and pepper. Heat the remaining tablespoon of olive oil in the pan over moderately high heat and pour in the egg mixture. Distribute the potato and artichokes evenly over the eggs and cook until the eggs are set around the edges.

Sprinkle the frittata with the cheese and place under the broiler. When the frittata is firm (but not dry) in the center, remove from the broiler. Let stand for 5 minutes, then remove to a serving platter. Sprinkle with parsley and serve.

Serves 4

Oven-Puffed Spinach Frittata

This one-dish entree can be prepared a day in advance, making fast work of any meal. Take care not to overcook the frittata or it will become tough and rubbery.

3 tablespoons unsalted butter, softened

Ten ½-inch-thick slices of French bread or firm white bread

4 large eggs

2 cups lowfat milk

2 teaspoons finely chopped fresh thyme or ½ teaspoon dried thyme

½ teaspoon salt

¼ teaspoon coarsely ground black pepper

1 pound fresh spinach, stemmed, washed, and torn into bite-sized pieces

½ pound Monterey Jack cheese, grated

LIGHTLY grease a 9- by 13-inch shallow baking pan.

Butter each slice of bread and cut into 1-inch cubes. Place half of the cubes in the pan. In a small bowl, whisk together the eggs, milk, thyme, salt, and pepper. Spread the spinach over the bread cubes and top with the remaining bread. Press down on the bread firmly. Pour the egg mixture over the bread and cover with the grated cheese. Cover, and refrigerate overnight.

Remove the frittata from the refrigerator and let stand at room temperature for 1 hour. Preheat the oven to 350°F.

Bake, uncovered, for 30 to 40 minutes, or until lightly browned and puffed. Serve immediately.

Serves 6 to 8

Eggplant, Red Pepper, and Parmesan Frittata

Be sure to allow the eggplant to soften and brown on all sides. This allows it to release its flavor.

1 medium eggplant (about 1 pound), cut into ¹/₂-inch cubes

¹/₂ cup finely chopped red bell pepper

2 tablespoons olive oil

¹/₄ teaspoon salt

¹/₄ teaspoon coarsely ground black pepper

¹/₄ teaspoon crushed red pepper

5 large eggs

3 cloves garlic, minced

¹/₄ cup finely chopped flat-leaf parsley

¹/₄ cup grated Parmigiano-Reggiano cheese

PLACE an oven rack 4 inches from the broiler unit and preheat the broiler.

In a medium bowl, toss together the eggplant, bell pepper, olive oil, salt, and peppers and transfer to a 9-inch ovenproof nonstick skillet. Cook over medium-high heat, stirring, until the eggplant is browned and softened, about 7 minutes. Meanwhile, in a small bowl, whisk together the eggs, garlic, and parsley and pour evenly over the vegetables. Do not stir. Cook until the outer 2 inches of the frittata are set.

Sprinkle the cheese over the eggs and place the pan under the broiler. When the frittata is puffed and golden and the center is just set, remove from the broiler. Loosen the bottom and sides of the frittata with a spatula and slide it onto a serving plate cheese side up. Serve immediately.

Serves 4

Soft Scrambled Eggs with Pasta

Whether assembled with last night's leftover noodles or freshly cooked ones, this is a fast and inventive method of combining two comfort foods. Add your favorite ingredients, such as sausage, salmon, bacon, sautéed red or green peppers, tomatoes, avocados, or other cheeses. I prefer long, thin pasta such as capellini or spaghettini, but spaghetti and linguine work well too.

½ pound dried cappellini or ¾ pound fresh

2 tablespoons extra-virgin olive oil

3 cloves garlic, minced

½ cup chopped scallions

8 large eggs, beaten

½ cup grated Parmigiano-Reggiano cheese

1 tablespoon finely chopped fresh marjoram

1 tablespoon finely chopped fresh chives

3 tablespoons finely chopped flat-leaf parsley

Coarsely ground black pepper

COOK the pasta in 3 to 4 quarts of salted water until barely tender, 7 to 8 minutes for dry, 3 to 4 minutes for fresh. Drain and set aside.

In a 12-inch nonstick skillet, heat the olive oil over medium heat and sauté the garlic until soft. Add the scallions and pasta and stir to coat the pasta with oil. Add the eggs, cheese, marjoram, chives, and 2 tablespoons of the parsley, and stir until the eggs are set and cling to the noodles, about 1 minute. Sprinkle with the remaining parsley, add pepper to taste, and serve.

Serves 4

Scrambled Eggs and Pan-Seared Mushrooms and Peppers

Cooked over high heat with little oil, these vegetables taste as if they were grilled. Wrap a warm flour tortilla around them and they become a portable meal.

1 tablespoon safflower oil

½ pound fresh mushrooms, thinly sliced

1 red bell pepper, seeded and cut into ¼-inch strips

1 jalapeño chili, seeded and finely minced

4 flour tortillas

6 large eggs

1 clove garlic, minced

½ cup coarsely chopped fresh cilantro

2 tablespoons finely chopped fresh chives

¼ teaspoon salt

⅛ teaspoon coarsely ground black pepper

2 tablespoons unsalted butter

Cilantro for garnish

PREHEAT the oven to 200°F.

In a large skillet over medium-high heat, heat the oil. Sauté the mushrooms, bell pepper, and jalapeño for 10 minutes, stirring frequently, until well browned and any liquid has evaporated. Remove the mushrooms and pepper to a plate.

Wrap the tortillas in a damp kitchen towel and heat in the oven until warm, about 10 minutes.

Meanwhile, whisk together the eggs, garlic, cilantro, chives, salt, and pepper. Wipe the skillet clean and place over medium heat. Add the butter and heat until it begins to sizzle. Pour in the egg mixture and stir until barely set. Add the mushroom mixture, scramble with the eggs, and divide among the warm tortillas. Garnish with cilantro and serve.

Serves 4

Baked Eggs on Pipérade

This version of pipérade takes advantage of early fall's abundance of colored peppers. Serve this with a salad of peppery greens such as chicory and arugula and chunks of country bread for a special breakfast or meatless light supper. Or spoon the pepper mixture on thick slices of toasted bread and serve with pasta or as an appetizer.

1/4 cup finely chopped onion

3 tablespoons extra-virgin olive oil

3 cloves garlic, minced

2 red bell peppers, cut into 1/2-inch dice

2 yellow bell peppers, cut into 1/2-inch dice

1 green bell pepper, cut into 1/2-inch dice

1/2 fresh jalapeño chili, seeded and minced

2 teaspoons chopped fresh thyme or 1 teaspoon dried thyme

2 teaspoons chopped fresh rosemary or 1 teaspoon crumbled dried rosemary

1/2 teaspoon dried oregano

Salt and coarsely ground black pepper

4 extra-large eggs

1/4 cup freshly grated Parmigiano-Reggiano cheese for garnish

In a 10-inch nonstick skillet over medium-high heat, sauté the onion in the olive oil until soft, about 5 minutes. Lower the heat, add the garlic, bell peppers, jalapeño, thyme, rosemary, and oregano, and cook until the vegetables are soft, about 10 minutes. Add salt and pepper to taste.

Preheat the oven to 375°F.

Lightly butter four 3/4-cup ramekins or shallow gratin dishes. Fill with approximately 1/2 cup of the pepper mixture, make an indentation in the center with the back of a spoon, and crack an egg into the indentation. Bake for 8 to 10 minutes or until the eggs are set. Sprinkle with the cheese and serve.

Serves 4

Poached Eggs in Ancho Chili and Tomato Sauce

Make this sauce a few days in advance to allow the flavors of the mild, slightly fruity ancho chili, the spices, and the tomatoes to develop.

2 ancho pasilla or dried chilies

One 14½-ounce can tomatoes with liquid, preferably chopped

2 cloves garlic, minced

1 teaspoon dried oregano

1 teaspoon sugar

1 teaspoon ground coriander

1 tablespoon lime juice

½ teaspoon salt

1 tablespoon white vinegar

4 large eggs

For Garnish

3 scallions, finely chopped with some green

½ cup chopped fresh cilantro

½ cup grated Parmigiano-Reggiano cheese

2 tablespoons sour cream (optional)

PLACE the chilies in a small bowl, pour 2 cups boiling water over them, and let stand for ½ hour. Stem and seed the chilies and place the skins in a blender with 1 cup of the soaking liquid. Puree on high speed until the mixture is thick and smooth. In a large saucepan, combine the puree, tomatoes, garlic, oregano, sugar, coriander, lime juice, and salt and simmer on low heat for 20 minutes. The sauce may be prepared up to this point 3 days ahead and kept covered and refrigerated. When ready to serve, bring the sauce to a simmer and divide among 4 shallow soup plates.

In a 10- or 12-inch skillet, bring 2 quarts of water to a boil. Add the vinegar and turn the heat to medium-low, so that bubbles form on the bottom of the pan. Break each egg into the water and cook for 3 to 4 minutes, or until the whites are opaque. Gently remove the eggs one at a time with a slotted spoon and place in the center of the prepared bowls of sauce. Sprinkle each with some of the scallions, cilantro, and cheese and top with sour cream, if using. Serve immediately with warm corn tortillas.

Serves 4

All-Day Omelets

*Avoid the temptation to overfill omelets;
about ¹/₄ cup of filling is enough without overwhelming the delicacy of the eggs.
Garnish them with heaps of fresh alfalfa, radish, or sunflower sprouts.*

For each omelet

2 large eggs

Pinch of salt and coarsely
    ground black pepper

2 teaspoons unsalted butter

In a small bowl, whisk together the eggs, salt, and pepper. In an 8-inch nonstick skillet over medium-high heat, melt the butter. When the butter sizzles, pour in the egg mixture. After about 5 seconds, using a fork or spatula, pull the cooked edges toward the center and allow the liquid to spill onto the hot pan. Cook for 20 seconds, then spread the filling in a line down the center. Tilt the pan and, using a spatula, roll one third of the omelet over the filling. Hold the pan over the serving plate so the unfolded side begins to slide out. Using the spatula, flip the omelet so the folded side folds over and the center is on the top.

Serves 1

Filling Variations

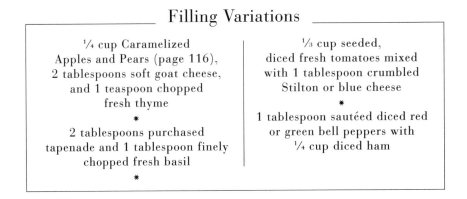

¹/₄ cup Caramelized
Apples and Pears (page 116),
2 tablespoons soft goat cheese,
and 1 teaspoon chopped
fresh thyme

✳

2 tablespoons purchased
tapenade and 1 tablespoon finely
chopped fresh basil

✳

¹/₃ cup seeded,
diced fresh tomatoes mixed
with 1 tablespoon crumbled
Stilton or blue cheese

✳

1 tablespoon sautéed diced red
or green bell peppers with
¹/₄ cup diced ham

Midnight Supper Eggs Calcutta

My *very grown-up kids still bring their friends to our traditional Easter egg-dyeing party, and I am always left with at least a dozen hard-cooked eggs. In this unusual egg dish, fragrant basmati is topped with hard-cooked eggs sautéed in aromatic Indian spices.*

1 tablespoon sesame seeds

1 teaspoon ground cumin

1 teaspoon cumin seeds

¼ teaspoon ground coriander

¼ teaspoon ground allspice

¼ teaspoon salt

¼ teaspoon coarsely ground black pepper

1 tablespoon olive oil

6 hard-cooked eggs, peeled and halved

½ cup finely chopped onion

1 cup chicken broth

1 tablespoon orange marmalade

2 tablespoons currants

Pinch of cayenne

4 cups cooked basmati or white long-grain rice

1 tablespoon finely chopped fresh cilantro mixed with 1 tablespoon drained capers, for garnish

PREHEAT the oven to 250°F.

In a small bowl, combine the sesame seeds, cumin, cumin seeds, coriander, allspice, salt, and pepper. Heat the oil in a 10-inch nonstick skillet over medium heat. Press the eggs, cut sides down, into the seed mixture and sauté the cut sides only in the oil. Cook until browned and crisp, about 5 minutes. Remove from the pan and keep warm in the oven.

In the same skillet, sauté the onion until soft and translucent, about 5 minutes. Stir in the broth, marmalade, currants, and cayenne and bring to a boil. Add the rice and stir until well coated with liquid and warmed through. Spoon the rice onto a serving platter and top with the eggs, cut sides up. Sprinkle with the cilantro-caper mixture and serve.

Serves 4 to 6

Caramelized Onion Tart

*P*ungent, sharp onions transform themselves *into something rich and sweet when cooked slowly. Make the cornmeal crust up to 2 days in advance and refrigerate. A simple green salad is all you need to complete the meal.*

For the Crust

1/3 cup yellow cornmeal

1 cup all-purpose flour

1/4 teaspoon salt

For the Filling

4 large onions (about 2 pounds)

1 tablespoon unsalted butter

2 tablespoons olive oil

1/2 teaspoon salt

1/4 teaspoon coarsely ground black pepper

1 tablespoon chopped fresh thyme or 1/2 teaspoon dried thyme

1/4 cup solid vegetable shortening

3 tablespoons unsalted butter

1 1/2 tablespoons all-purpose flour

Few gratings fresh nutmeg

2 large eggs

3/4 cup milk

1 cup grated Swiss or Gruyère cheese

2 tablespoons grated Parmigiano-Reggiano cheese

To make the crust: In a food processor fitted with a metal blade, finely grind the cornmeal. Add the flour and salt and pulse to combine. Cut the shortening and butter into small pieces and add to the flour mixture. Pulse until the mixture is the texture of coarse meal. Add the water and pulse again just to moisten. The mixture should hold together when pressed between 2 fingers. Turn out onto a lightly floured surface and knead several times. Cover tightly with plastic wrap and chill 1 hour or up to 2 days. When ready to bake the tart, roll the dough to 1/4-inch thickness and carefully fit it into a 9-inch tart pan with removable bottom. Place a rack in the lowest part of the oven and preheat to 400°F.

Peel the onions and cut into quarters. Place in the bowl of a food processor fitted with a metal blade in 2 batches and pulse to chop.

In a large nonstick skillet, melt the butter with the olive oil and sauté the onions, stirring often, over moderately low heat for 40 to 50 minutes, until soft and golden brown. Remove from the heat and stir in the salt, pepper, thyme, flour, and nutmeg.

In a small bowl, whisk together the eggs and milk. Stir in 1/2 cup of Swiss cheese and the onion mixture. Sprinkle the remaining cheese over the prepared crust and pour in the filling. Sprinkle the top with the Parmesan and bake for 30 to 35 minutes. Remove from the oven and allow to rest for 5 minutes. Remove outer rim of pan and serve.

Serves 6

Provençal Sweet Spinach Tart
with Pine Nuts

In southern France this quiche-like tart contains crystallized fruits and is served as a dessert. I add raisins and fresh chèvre instead for breakfast or a light supper. The pastry can be made a day ahead and refrigerated.

For the Pastry

2 cups all-purpose flour

½ teaspoon salt

½ cup (1 stick) cold unsalted butter, cut into tablespoons

2 tablespoons solid vegetable shortening

1 large egg, lightly beaten

For the Filling

1½ pounds fresh spinach, washed and stemmed

2 cups milk

⅓ cup sugar

4 large eggs

2 tablespoons all-purpose flour

¼ teaspoon salt

2 teaspoons finely chopped lemon zest

½ cup golden raisins, chopped

¼ cup pine nuts, lightly toasted

2 ounces soft goat cheese

To make the pastry: Place the flour and salt in a food processor and pulse to combine. Add the butter and shortening and pulse until the mixture resembles coarse meal. Add the egg and 2 tablespoons of ice water and process just until the mixture holds together when pressed between 2 fingers. Form the dough into a ball and wrap tightly in plastic wrap. Chill in the refrigerator for several hours or up to 2 days.

To assemble the tart: Roll the dough out into a circle ¼ inch thick. Fit into a 9-inch quiche dish or pie pan. Trim off the excess dough and fold into a decorative edge. Set aside.

Preheat the oven to 400°F.

In a medium saucepan over medium heat, steam the spinach in the water that is clinging to its leaves for 2 minutes. Cool. Drain and squeeze out the excess water with your hands, chop the spinach finely, and wrap in paper towels and squeeze again. In a medium bowl, whisk together the milk, sugar, eggs, flour, salt, and zest. Stir in the spinach and raisins and pour into the prepared pastry. Sprinkle with the pine nuts and goat cheese and bake for 35 to 40 minutes, until the pastry is golden and the filling is set. Cool 10 to 15 minutes before serving.

Serves 6

Creamy Farina and Artichoke Soufflé

Best known by the brand name Cream
of Wheat, farina is nothing more than granules of wheat that readily absorb liquid
and cook to a creamy consistency. Although it is almost exclusively considered a
breakfast cereal, I have found that it makes a terrific base for a soufflé for any meal,
especially when combined with a little Parmesan and artichoke hearts.

2 cups lowfat or whole milk

$\frac{1}{2}$ teaspoon salt

$\frac{1}{3}$ cup farina

4 large eggs, separated

Two 6-ounce jars marinated
   artichoke hearts, drained
   and pureed in a food
   processor

$\frac{1}{2}$ cup grated Parmigiano-
   Reggiano cheese

1 teaspoon finely chopped
   fresh thyme or $\frac{1}{2}$ teaspoon
   dried thyme

PLACE an oven rack in the center of the oven and preheat to 350°F. Generously butter a
2-quart soufflé dish.

In a medium saucepan, combine the milk and salt and bring to a boil. Slowly stir in
the farina. Lower the heat and cook, stirring constantly, until the mixture is thick and all
of the liquid has been absorbed. Stir in the egg yolks, artichoke hearts, cheese, and thyme
and set aside.

In a large bowl, beat the egg whites until they hold stiff peaks. Fold one-third of the
whites into the artichoke mixture, then quickly fold in the remaining whites. Pour the
mixture into the soufflé dish, smoothing the top with a rubber spatula, and bake for 45 to
50 minutes, until puffed and golden brown. Serve immediately.

Serves 4 to 6

Apple and Sage Cheese Soufflé

T*o appreciate this beautiful puffed egg concoction, everyone must be seated at the table before the soufflé comes out of the oven. The base, or roux, can be stirred together hours before, but the whisked egg whites should be folded into the mixture just before it goes into the oven. For a splendid breakfast or lunch, serve with slices of melon or a salad and a Blueberry Buttermilk Muffin (page 97).*

3 tablespoons unsalted butter

4 tablespoons all-purpose flour

1 cup milk, warmed

$\frac{1}{2}$ teaspoon salt

1 teaspoon crumbled dried sage (not ground sage)

2 tablespoons sugar

4 large eggs, separated

1 cup loosely packed grated extra-sharp Cheddar or Gorgonzola cheese

2 medium apples, peeled and finely chopped in a food processor

PLACE an oven rack in the center of the oven and preheat to 375°F. Lightly butter a 2-quart soufflé dish.

In a medium saucepan over medium heat, melt the butter. Add the flour gradually and whisk until a smooth paste forms. Slowly add the milk and continue whisking, smoothing out any lumps, until a thick sauce is formed, 2 to 3 minutes. Remove from the heat. Whisk in the salt, sage, sugar, egg yolks, cheese, and the apples. Set aside.

In a large bowl, beat the egg whites until stiff but not dry. Fold one-third of the whites into the yolk mixture, then quickly fold in the remaining whites. Pour the mixture into the soufflé dish, smoothing the top with a rubber spatula. Turn the oven to 350°F. and bake 45 to 55 minutes, until puffed and golden brown. The center will be very soft but will firm up as the soufflé cools. Serve immediately.

Serves 6

Huevos Ranchitos

A *bright green tomatillo-based sauce takes the place of the red "ranchero" sauce traditionally served with this Tex-Mex classic. I poach the eggs instead of frying them and use buttery California avocados.*

One 18-ounce can whole tomatillos or 10 medium fresh

2 tablespoons lime juice

2 cloves garlic, minced

2 tablespoons finely chopped onion

½ teaspoon salt

¼ teaspoon sugar

¼ teaspoon ground cumin

1 cup cilantro leaves

1 jalapeño chili, seeded and minced

½ ripe avocado, thickly sliced

♦

¼ cup safflower oil

8 corn tortillas

2 tablespoons white vinegar

4 large eggs

1½ cups grated Cheddar cheese

2 tablespoons cumin seeds, toasted

1 ripe avocado, peeled and thinly sliced

½ cup cilantro leaves

DRAIN the tomatillos and place in a food processor fitted with a metal blade. (If using fresh tomatillos, remove the papery skins and cook in boiling water for 20 minutes and drain.) Add the lime juice, garlic, onion, salt, sugar, cumin, and cilantro and process until pureed. Add the jalapeño and avocado, pulse to combine, and set aside. The sauce can be made 1 day ahead and refrigerated. Makes 1½ cups.

In a 12-inch skillet, heat 1 tablespoon of the oil over medium heat and add 2 tortillas. Heat until softened, drain on paper towels, and repeat with the remaining tortillas.

To poach the eggs, place water in a skillet or shallow pan to a depth of 2½ inches. Add the vinegar and heat over medium-high heat. When the water is at a low boil, carefully break the eggs into the pan and cook just until the whites become opaque, about 3 minutes.

Meanwhile, preheat the broiler. Place 2 tortillas overlapping by 2 inches in the center of 4 plates. Remove each poached egg with a slotted spoon and place on the overlapping portion of the tortillas. Sprinkle the grated cheese equally among the plates and top each with 3 tablespoons of the sauce and about a teaspoon of the cumin seeds. Place under the broiler just to melt the cheese and garnish with avocado slices and cilantro.

Serves 4

Pancakes and Waffles

Universally loved, positively versatile, pancakes and waffles are good enough to eat morning, noon, and night and anytime in between. If just hearing the words *pancakes* and *waffles* makes you salivate, why indulge in them only at breakfast? As simple to make as a plate of pasta, sweet or savory pancakes and waffles are perfectly suited to impromptu lunches, weeknight dinners, and midnight snacks. ✳ Think of pancakes and waffles as canvases, whether dressed on the outside with stewed or fresh fruits and fruited syrups (see page 137) or from the inside out with savory ingredients such as potatoes, zucchini, fennel, and parsley. Press an ordinary peanut butter sandwich in a waffle iron and drizzle with honey for a special treat. Whether you crave puffy, golden-hued Honey Whole-Wheat Pancakes (page 24) drenched in warm maple syrup, hearty Wild Rice and Toasted Pecan Waffles (page 31) with a dollop of cool yogurt cheese, or Brownie Waffles (page 32) slathered with raspberry jam, there are pancakes and waffles here to satisfy your fancy in the time it takes to open a box of cereal, unscrew the peanut butter jar, or bring pasta to a boil.

Basic Pancakes

These are the pancakes for which soft butter and lots of warm maple syrup were made. Enjoy!

1 cup all-purpose flour

2 tablespoons sugar

1 teaspoon baking powder

1/4 teaspoon salt

3 large eggs, lightly beaten

3/4 cup milk

2 tablespoons unsalted butter, melted

PREHEAT the oven to 250°F.

Stir the flour, sugar, baking powder, and salt together in a mixing bowl. Make a well in the center and add the eggs, milk, and butter. Lightly mix just until all the dry ingredients are moistened. Heat a 12-inch nonstick skillet or griddle over medium heat. Spoon scant 1/4 cups of batter onto the skillet and cook until bubbles start to appear on the surface. Turn the pancakes and cook briefly on the other side. Keep the pancakes warm in the oven while using up the remaining batter.

Makes twelve 3-inch pancakes

Variations

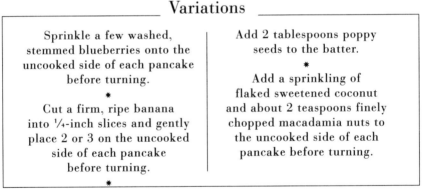

Sprinkle a few washed, stemmed blueberries onto the uncooked side of each pancake before turning.

*

Cut a firm, ripe banana into 1/4-inch slices and gently place 2 or 3 on the uncooked side of each pancake before turning.

*

Add 2 tablespoons poppy seeds to the batter.

*

Add a sprinkling of flaked sweetened coconut and about 2 teaspoons finely chopped macadamia nuts to the uncooked side of each pancake before turning.

Blue Cornmeal Pancakes with Honey Apple Syrup

Soft and sweetly fragrant of corn, blue cornmeal turns the shade of the winter sky at dusk when mixed with liquids. Bubbles will not appear on top when the pancakes are ready to be flipped. Turn them when the edges look firm.

1 cup blue cornmeal

2 tablespoons all-purpose flour

½ teaspoon baking soda

¼ teaspoon salt

1 cup buttermilk

3 tablespoons unsalted butter, melted

1 large egg

STIR together the cornmeal, flour, baking soda, and salt in a mixing bowl. Make a well in the center and add the buttermilk, butter, and egg. Whisk the ingredients together until well blended. The mixture will be the consistency of thick cake batter. Thin with a little more buttermilk if necessary. Heat a 12-inch nonstick skillet or a butter-filmed griddle over medium heat. Pour scant ¼ cups of batter onto the skillet and cook until the edges look firm. Turn the pancakes and cook 1 to 2 minutes longer. Serve immediately with Honey Apple Syrup (page 141).

Makes twelve 3½-inch pancakes

Honey Whole-Wheat Pancakes

This is the pancake batter to make when your child has a slumber party or you have weekend guests. Stir a cup of fresh blueberries or peaches or other fruit in season (peel and dice peaches) into the batter. Serve these wholesome pancakes with Sweet Orange and Banana Syrup (page 142).

1 cup whole-wheat flour	3 tablespoons honey
¾ cup all-purpose flour	3 tablespoons safflower oil
⅔ cup yellow cornmeal	3 large eggs
1 tablespoon baking powder	2 cups buttermilk
1 teaspoon baking soda	1 cup fresh blueberries or peaches (optional)
½ teaspoon salt	

PREHEAT the oven to 250°F.

In a large bowl, stir together the flours, cornmeal, baking powder, baking soda, and salt. Make a well in the center and add the honey, oil, eggs, and buttermilk. Stir together just until moistened. Add fruit, if using. Heat a 12-inch nonstick skillet or griddle over medium heat. Pour scant ¼ cups of batter onto the skillet and cook until tops are bubbly. Turn the pancakes and cook until lightly browned. Keep the pancakes warm in the oven while using up the remaining batter. Serve with warm syrup.

Makes eighteen 3-inch pancakes

Yogurt Pancakes

Yogurt has a tenderizing effect on this batter; there's no need to add beaten egg whites to these perfect light pancakes. Cook these a little slower and longer. The butter should be the consistency of softly whipped cream. If it is too thick, add a little milk.

2 cups all-purpose flour	1 tablespoon sugar
1 teaspoon baking soda	2 large eggs
¼ teaspoon salt	2 cups plain lowfat yogurt

PREHEAT the oven to 250° F.

In a large bowl, stir together the flour, baking soda, salt, and sugar. Make a well in the center and beat in the eggs and yogurt with a wooden spoon. Heat a 12-inch nonstick skillet or griddle over medium heat. Pour scant $^1/_4$ cups of the batter onto the skillet and cook until bubbles start to appear on top. Turn the pancakes and cook briefly on the opposite side to brown lightly. Keep the pancakes warm in the oven while using up the remaining batter.

Makes twelve to fourteen 3-inch pancakes

Rice-Flour Pancakes

Fine, powdery rice flour gives these pancakes a soft, light texture. For those who are allergic to wheat, they offer a delicious alternative to cornmeal or oat pancakes. Rice flour can often be purchased in health food stores or Middle Eastern markets.

1 cup buttermilk	$^3/_4$ cup rice flour
1 large egg	$^1/_2$ teaspoon salt
3 tablespoons unsalted butter, melted	1 teaspoon baking soda
	1 teaspoon sugar

PREHEAT the oven to 250°F.

In a medium bowl, whisk together the buttermilk, egg, and butter. In a small bowl, stir together the flour, salt, baking soda, and sugar. Add the dry mixture to the buttermilk mixture and stir until moistened. The batter will still be lumpy.

Brush a light film of butter on a 12-inch nonstick skillet or griddle and heat over medium-high heat. Pour scant $^1/_4$ cups of batter onto the skillet and cook until a few bubbles break on the surface. Turn the pancakes and cook briefly on the other side. Keep the pancakes warm in the oven while using up the remaining batter. Serve with warm syrup or jam.

Makes twelve 4-inch pancakes

Potato and Fennel Pancakes

Sweet and delicate anise-flavored fennel enlivens the potato in these savory pancakes. Work quickly after stirring all of the ingredients together, as the potato exudes juices that will thin the batter. Top the pancakes with slices of smoked salmon and a dab of sour cream, and you'll think you are breakfasting at a luxury hotel.

1 large baking potato, peeled and cut into $1/2$-inch pieces

$2/3$ cup finely chopped fennel, including some of the green

2 tablespoons finely chopped onion

$1/4$ cup all-purpose flour

1 large egg

$1/2$ teaspoon salt

$1/8$ teaspoon coarsely ground black pepper

2 tablespoons safflower oil

$1/4$ pound smoked salmon, thinly sliced

$1/4$ cup finely chopped fresh chives

$1/4$ cup crème fraîche or sour cream

PREHEAT the oven to 250°F.

In a medium bowl combine the potato, fennel, onion, flour, egg, salt, and pepper and stir to combine. In a heavy 10-inch skillet, preferably cast iron, over medium-high heat, heat the oil. Drop $1/4$ cup of the potato mixture onto the skillet and spread into a 4-inch circle with the back of a spoon or spatula. Cook for 4 to 5 minutes per side, until browned and crispy. Keep the pancakes warm in the oven while making the remaining pancakes.

To serve, lay several strips of smoked salmon on each pancake, sprinkle with chopped chives, and top with a tablespoon of crème fraîche or sour cream.

Makes eight 4-inch pancakes

Savory Zucchini Pancakes

My *family often requests these vegetable pancakes in the summer when we're cooking on the grill, but I have also served them for lunch and Sunday supper.*

4 medium zucchini, grated

1 baking potato, peeled and grated

¼ cup finely chopped red onion

1 teaspoon salt

2 large eggs, lightly beaten

½ teaspoon dried thyme or 1 teaspoon chopped fresh thyme

½ teaspoon paprika

¼ cup all-purpose flour

¼ teaspoon coarsely ground black pepper

4 tablespoons safflower oil

IN a medium bowl, toss together the zucchini, potato, onion, and salt. Transfer the mixture to a strainer and drain for 30 minutes, then press down to squeeze dry. Return the mixture to the bowl and combine with the eggs, thyme, paprika, flour, and pepper.

Preheat the oven to 250°F.

Heat the oil in a 12-inch skillet and drop ¼ cup of batter onto the pan, spreading it into a 3-inch disc with the back of a metal spoon. Cook until lightly browned, then turn and cook until the other side is golden brown. Keep the pancakes warm in the oven while you cook the remaining ones. Top with a dollop of plain yogurt or sour cream and serve immediately.

Makes twelve 3-inch pancakes

Tomato Basil Pancakes

Two of the best flavors to come out of a summer garden, tomatoes and basil bespeckle these savory pancakes. For a midday meal, serve them with grilled Italian sausages.

1¼ cups all-purpose flour

⅓ cup cornmeal, preferably white

1 teaspoon baking powder

1 teaspoon baking soda

1 tablespoon sugar

½ teaspoon salt

3 large ripe tomatoes, seeded and diced

2 large eggs, beaten

2 tablespoons safflower oil

1½ cups buttermilk

½ cup finely chopped flat-leaf parsley

3 tablespoons chopped fresh basil

2 tablespoons finely chopped scallions

Dash of Tabasco sauce

Plain lowfat yogurt and finely chopped scallions for garnish

In a medium bowl, stir together the flour, cornmeal, baking powder, baking soda, sugar, and salt. Add the tomatoes, eggs, oil, buttermilk, parsley, basil, scallions, and Tabasco and stir to combine.

Brush a light film of butter on a 12-inch nonstick skillet or griddle and heat over medium-high heat. Pour ⅓ cups of the batter onto the skillet and cook until bubbles appear on top of the surface. Turn the pancakes and brown on the other side. Top with a dollop of yogurt and sprinkle with scallions. Serve with sautéed slices of ham or Canadian bacon.

Makes twelve 3-inch pancakes
Serves 4

Thin and Crispy Cornmeal Crêpes

A cross between a traditional crêpe and a tortilla, these whisper-thin pancakes are very versatile. Top them with fresh fruit and syrups or wrap them around sautéed sausages and potatoes. Use them for blintzes too, spread with ricotta and drizzled with Pineapple Jalapeño Syrup.

1⅓ cups lowfat or whole milk	⅔ cup yellow cornmeal
3 large eggs	¼ teaspoon salt
½ cup all-purpose flour	1 teaspoon sugar

POUR the milk, eggs, flour, cornmeal, salt, and sugar into a blender and process until well combined. Pour into a bowl. Stir the batter before making each crêpe since cornmeal sinks to the bottom.

Lightly brush a 6-inch nonstick skillet or crêpe pan with butter and heat over medium-high heat. Pour 2 to 3 tablespoons of batter into the pan and tilt the pan to spread the batter thinly over the entire surface. Cook until set. Turn the crêpe with a metal spatula and cook until light brown splotches appear on the bottom, about 1 minute. Remove to a plate and fold into quarters. Repeat with the remaining batter, brushing the pan with butter as necessary.

Serve with Ham and Sweet Potato Hash (page 46) or Pineapple Jalapeño Syrup (page 143).

Makes sixteen 6-inch crêpes

Popover Pancake

This traditional German oven-baked pancake lends itself to sweet and savory toppings. I use nonfat milk, which I secretly think makes it rise better!

For the Pancake

2 tablespoons unsalted butter

3 large eggs

2½ cups nonfat milk

⅔ cup all-purpose flour

½ teaspoon salt

For the Fruit Topping

2 ounces soft goat cheese, crumbled

2 cups raspberries

½ cup sifted powdered sugar

For the Savory Topping

½ pound mild Italian sausages, casings removed

1 large tomato, seeded and diced

½ cup grated Parmigiano-Reggiano cheese

2 tablespoons finely chopped flat-leaf parsley

PLACE an oven rack in the lower third of the oven and preheat to 450°F.

In a 9- or 10-inch ovenproof skillet over medium heat, melt the butter, then remove from the heat. Beat the eggs on high speed in a blender for 1 minute. Add the milk, flour, and salt and continue beating for 1 more minute until blended and foamy. Immediately pour the mixture into the hot skillet. Place in the oven and bake for 20 minutes. Reduce the heat to 350°F. and continue baking for 10 minutes, until golden brown and well puffed.

Sprinkle with goat cheese and raspberries and dust with the powdered sugar. Or use the savory topping.

To make the savory topping: In a 10-inch skillet over medium-high heat, sauté the sausages while the pancake is baking. Drain off the fat and juices and stir in the tomato. Spoon the sausage mixture on the pancake, and sprinkle with cheese and parsley.

Serve immediately.

Serves 4

Wild Rice and Toasted Pecan Waffles

Toasted pecans enhance the wonderfully nutty flavor and chewy texture of wild rice. Top these waffles with warm maple or fruited syrup for breakfast or Caramelized Apples and Pears (page 116) for a perfect light supper.

1 cup pecans, finely chopped

1 cup all-purpose flour

¼ cup cornmeal, preferably white

2 cups cooked wild rice, well drained

2 teaspoons baking powder

1 tablespoon sugar

1 teaspoon baking soda

¼ teaspoon salt

1½ cups buttermilk

2 large eggs

¼ cup safflower oil

PREHEAT the oven to 350°F. and preheat a waffle iron.

Spread the pecans on a baking sheet and toast in the oven until fragrant, about 10 minutes. Set aside to cool.

In a large mixing bowl, stir together the flour, cornmeal, rice, baking powder, sugar, baking soda, and salt. Add the buttermilk, eggs, and oil and stir until the batter is smooth. Pour approximately ¾ cup of the batter onto the waffle iron and cook according to the manufacturer's instructions. Serve hot with fruit or syrup.

Makes six 8-inch waffles

Fannie Farmer's Raised Waffles

The first cookbook I owned was a 1957 edition of The Fannie Farmer Cookbook. *Eventually I replaced it with Marion Cunningham's revised version in 1984, although I continued to refer to the old book mostly for my handwritten notes in the margins and one of my favorite recipes that was omitted in the revision. I reprint it here because I have yet to find another waffle that comes close to its crisp, light texture, ease of preparation, or tantalizing yeasty aroma.*

½ cup warm water (105° to 110°F.)

One ¼-ounce package dry yeast

2 cups warm milk (about 100°F.)

½ cup (1 stick) unsalted butter, melted

1 teaspoon salt

1 teaspoon sugar

2 cups all-purpose flour

2 large eggs

¼ teaspoon baking soda

POUR the water into a large mixing bowl and sprinkle in the yeast. Allow to stand for 5 minutes. Whisk in the milk, butter, salt, sugar, and flour until no lumps appear in the batter. Cover the bowl with plastic wrap and leave at room temperature overnight.

Preheat an electric waffle iron. Whisk the eggs and baking soda into the batter. It will be very thin. Pour ½ to ¾ cup of batter onto the hot waffle iron and bake until golden and crisp. Serve with fruit or syrup.

The batter will keep, covered, in the refrigerator for several days.

Makes 8 waffles

Brownie Waffles

Here's a way for confirmed chocoholics to get a chocolate fix for breakfast. These waffles are really brownies baked in a waffle iron. Spread them with Yogurt Cheese (page 140) or raspberry jam.

<table>
<tr><td>¾ cup sugar</td><td>2 large eggs</td></tr>
</table>

¾ cup sugar

½ cup (1 stick) unsalted
   butter, at room temperature

2 squares (2 ounces)
   unsweetened chocolate,
   melted

1 teaspoon vanilla extract

2 large eggs

½ cup milk

1 teaspoon baking powder

¾ cup all-purpose flour

½ cup whole-wheat flour

Pinch of salt

PREHEAT a waffle iron and brush lightly with oil, if necessary.

In the bowl of an electric mixer, cream the sugar and butter until light and fluffy. Add the chocolate, vanilla, eggs, and milk and mix on medium speed until smooth, about 3 minutes. Add the baking powder, flours, and salt and mix just until incorporated.

Drop about 1 rounded tablespoon of batter onto each quarter of the waffle iron and bake just until the steaming stops, about 2 minutes. The waffle will be soft and flabby, but will become crisp as it cools.

Serve immediately with yogurt cheese, jam, or syrup, or allow to cool to room temperature and dust with powdered sugar.

Makes about eight 6-inch waffles

Quick Baked Blintz

Make blintzes in a snap using flour tortillas in place of homemade crêpes. These are filled with ricotta and jam, but they can be filled with your favorite sweet or savory filling.

½ cup lowfat ricotta cheese

¼ cup raspberry or
   strawberry jam

Two 8-inch flour tortillas, at
   room temperature

2 tablespoons milk

2 teaspoons sugar

PREHEAT the oven to 425°F.

Spread half of the ricotta and jam down the center of each tortilla. Fold the sides over the filling so that they overlap. Start at one end and fold up the blintz. Brush each with the milk and sprinkle with sugar. Place on a greased shallow baking pan and bake for 12 to 14 minutes, until golden. Cool slightly before serving.

Makes 2 blintzes

Honeyed French Toast Sandwich

I *love French toast and am always tucking interesting things between 2 eggy slices. Think of it next time you make yourself a sandwich.*

3 large eggs

½ cup lowfat milk

¼ cup honey

2 tablespoons all-purpose flour

½ teaspoon baking powder

4 slices firm-textured white or egg bread

1 tablespoon safflower oil

1 tablespoon unsalted butter

¼ cup Yogurt Cheese (page 140) or ricotta cheese

1 cup thinly sliced strawberries

Powdered sugar

Maple syrup (optional)

IN a shallow dish, whisk together the eggs, milk, honey, flour, and baking powder. Press each piece of bread into the mixture and allow to soak for several minutes. Using a spatula, turn and allow the other side to soak.

In a 12-inch skillet over medium-high heat, heat the oil and butter. Using a spatula, lift the bread from the batter into the pan and brown on both sides. Spread the yogurt cheese on 2 of the slices and distribute the strawberries evenly over the cheese. Top with the remaining slices, sprinkle with the powdered sugar, and serve. Pass maple syrup, if desired.

Makes 2 sandwiches

Variation

To make a ham sandwich:

After browning, spread one side of each of the 2 slices with Dijon mustard, add thinly sliced ham, and top with the remaining toast. Serve hot.

Toasted Almond French Toast

One of the great treats of my childhood summers in New Jersey was a visit to the Good Humor truck. This recipe is inspired by the toasted almond bar, which always seemed more exotic than fruit Popsicles. Make this out-of-the ordinary toast for someone special.

1 cup sliced unblanched
    almonds

3 large eggs

1 cup lowfat milk

2 tablespoons flour

1/2 teaspoon baking powder

1/4 teaspoon salt

1 teaspoon vanilla extract

1/2 teaspoon almond extract

Six 1/2-inch slices of French
    bread

2 tablespoons unsalted butter

2 tablespoons safflower oil

PREHEAT the oven to 350°F.

Spread the almonds on a baking sheet and toast in the oven for 10 minutes, until lightly browned and fragrant. Remove to a plate and set aside to cool.

In a medium bowl, whisk together the eggs, milk, flour, baking powder, salt, and vanilla and almond extracts. Dip both sides of the bread into the egg mixture and place in a shallow pan. Pour the remaining mixture over the bread slices and allow to soak for 1 hour or cover and refrigerate overnight.

Preheat the oven to 250°F.

In a 12-inch skillet over moderate heat, melt the butter and oil. When the butter sizzles, sprinkle the almonds in the skillet, press one side of the bread firmly onto the almonds and cook, almond side down, until well browned, about 5 minutes. Turn and brown the other side. Keep the toast warm in the oven and continue with the slices. Serve warm with syrup or fruit.

Makes 6 toasts

Preceding Page
Fresh Fig, Prosciutto, and Parmesan Sandwich

Above
Berries and Spinach Salad

Left
Salmonburger

Sweet Potato and Black Pepper Biscuits

Top
Zucchini and Feta Frittata

Above
Honeyed French Toast Sandwich

Left
Plum Kuchen

Tea and Fruit Bread and Cider

Multi-Grain, Multi-Seed, Multi-Nut Granola

Next Page
Pineapple Papaya Soother

House Specials

When I was growing up, my family ate the biggest meal on Sunday just after church. Of course, we thought we would never be hungry again after the feast, but the pangs would inevitably set in later that night. These "house specials" are inspired by the dishes we tossed together for our late suppers. They often took the form of omelets, rarebit, or hash, a great catchall dish that can be a meal by itself or paired with meat or eggs. To make hash, start with cooked potatoes, then use your imagination. Turkey Hash (page 45) lets you savor the flavors of Thanksgiving any time of year. Throw in cranberries, pearl onions, turnips, stuffing, and diced turkey and you have a spectacular breakfast or supper. With almost no planning, the Fresh Fig, Prosciutto, and Parmesan Sandwiches (page 48) can be the hit of Sunday brunch. ✳ If breakfast time is stressful, grab a hearty muffin and plan to use your breakfast ingredients at lunch or dinner. A poached egg served on top of a Crunchy Crab Cake (page 52) makes a hearty dinner. If you have craved diner-style hash browns all day, toss together the Herbed Potatoes and Spinach Stir-Fry (page 40) for supper and eat the leftovers the next morning.

Saffron Polenta with Ratatouille and Parmesan

The possibilities for polenta are endless. Serve it with sausage or bacon and a green salad for a quick weekday supper or broil it and top with a poached egg for a unique breakfast.

3½ cups milk

3½ cups water

½ teaspoon saffron

½ teaspoon salt

1½ cups coarsely ground cornmeal

½ cup grated pecorino or Parmesan cheese

6 tablespoons olive oil

4 cloves garlic, minced

1 medium eggplant (about 1 pound), cut into ½-inch dice

½ cup whole basil leaves

2 medium zucchini (about ¾ pound), cut into 1-inch dice

1 small onion, finely chopped

8 plum tomatoes (about 1 pound), coarsely chopped

½ teaspoon salt

¼ teaspoon crushed red pepper

⅛ teaspoon coarsely ground black pepper

Grated Parmesan cheese for garnish

To make the polenta: In a medium saucepan, combine the milk and water and bring to a boil. Stir in the saffron and salt. Slowly stir in the cornmeal and cook, stirring, until the mixture is as thick as mashed potatoes and pulls cleanly away from the sides of the pan, about 20 minutes. Stir in the cheese and immediately pour into a 13- by 9-inch baking pan and smooth the top. Allow to come to room temperature, then cover and refrigerate.

To make the ratatouille: In a 12-inch nonstick skillet over high heat, heat 3 tablespoons of the olive oil and half of the garlic. Add the eggplant and cook, stirring until it is translucent, about 30 minutes. Remove to an oven-proof bowl and cover with half of the basil leaves. Heat the remaining olive oil and garlic in the skillet and add the zucchini and onion. Cook, stirring, until the zucchini is lightly browned. Add the tomatoes and cook until the zucchini is tender and the tomatoes give off their juices. Stir in the salt, red pepper, and black pepper. Layer the vegetables on top of the eggplant and cover with the remaining basil leaves. Set aside to cool, then refrigerate, covered, overnight.

Preheat the oven to 350°F. Cut the polenta into 2½-inch rounds or rectangles. Film a large nonstick skillet with oil and sauté both sides of the polenta until golden and crispy. Keep warm in the oven. Meanwhile, warm the ratatouille in the oven for 20 minutes, stirring once. Place a slice of polenta on each plate and spoon the ratatouille around it. Sprinkle with cheese and serve.

Serves 8

Warm Mushrooms and Shallots
on Parmesan Toast

Juicy, succulent wild mushrooms are as gratifying to eat as grilled meat, and far more healthy. If you need a red meat fix, add 3 ounces of finely chopped sautéed pancetta to the mushroom mixture. This can also be served spooned on rounds of Saffron Polenta (page 38).

Four ½-inch slices of rye or whole-wheat bread, lightly toasted

5 tablespoons olive oil

½ cup freshly grated Parmigiano-Reggiano cheese

1 ounce dried shiitake or porcini mushrooms

6 shallots, chopped

3 cloves garlic, minced

½ pound fresh wild mushrooms, wiped clean and thinly sliced

½ pound small white button mushrooms, halved

2 teaspoons chopped fresh thyme or 1 teaspoon dried thyme

1 tablespoon sherry vinegar (optional)

½ cup chicken broth

Salt and coarsely ground black pepper

2 tablespoons chopped flat-leaf parsley

Brush each toast lightly with olive oil and sprinkle with 1 tablespoon of the cheese and set aside.

Bring 1 cup of water to a boil and pour it over the dried mushrooms. Let them soak for 20 minutes. Strain the soaking liquid through a very fine mesh strainer to remove any sand and reserve. Trim the stem from each mushroom and slice the cap into ¼-inch strips.

Heat 2 tablespoons of the olive oil in a 9- or 10-inch heavy skillet over medium heat. Add the shallots, garlic, and dried mushrooms and sauté for 6 to 8 minutes. Add the remaining olive oil and fresh mushrooms and sauté until they begin to exude their juices. Stir in the soaking liquid, thyme, vinegar, if using, and chicken broth. Reduce the heat to a simmer and continue cooking for 8 to 10 minutes, stirring often, until the mushrooms are tender and most of the liquid has evaporated. Season to taste with salt and pepper.

Spoon the mushroom mixture equally over the prepared toasts, sprinkle with the remaining cheese and the parsley, and serve.

Serves 4

Herbed Potatoes and Spinach Stir-Fry

Warmed tart goat cheese and fragrant rosemary work wonders with potatoes, scallions, and spinach in this vegetarian hash. Gorgonzola or a mild blue cheese can substitute for the goat cheese if you choose.

2 pounds red-skinned potatoes, unpeeled, cut into 1-inch dice

2 tablespoons olive oil

1 tablespoon dried rosemary or 2 tablespoons fresh rosemary

1/4 teaspoon salt

1/4 teaspoon coarsely ground black pepper

12 ounces fresh spinach, washed and stemmed

3 scallions, thinly sliced with some of the green

2 ounces grated fresh goat cheese

2 tablespoons finely chopped flat-leaf parsley for garnish

Bring a medium saucepan full of lightly salted water to a boil. Add the potatoes, turn the heat to medium, and continue to cook for 10 minutes, until the potatoes are barely tender. Drain and cool to room temperature or cover and refrigerate overnight.

Heat the oil in a large sauté pan or wok over high heat. Add the potatoes and cook until they are crisp and lightly browned. Add the rosemary, salt, and pepper. Fold the spinach into the potatoes and cook until the spinach begins to wilt. Sprinkle with the scallions and goat cheese and cook for just 2 minutes more to soften the cheese. Garnish with parsley and serve immediately.

Serves 4

Tomato Potato Galette

This simple savory pie is my answer to quiche. I created it using grated potatoes for the crust and no cream or eggs in the filling. Use only the ripest fresh tomatoes.

5 medium red-skinned potatoes, washed and grated

¼ teaspoon salt

¼ teaspoon coarsely ground black pepper

3 cloves garlic, minced

1 teaspoon chopped fresh thyme or ½ teaspoon dried thyme

1 tablespoon white wine vinegar

1 large egg

3 tablespoons olive oil

2 to 3 large, firm, but very ripe, tomatoes (preferably beefsteak), sliced

3 ounces gorgonzola, chèvre, or feta cheese, crumbled

10 whole basil leaves, cut into ¼-inch strips

PREHEAT the oven to 400°F. and place the rack in the lowest position.

Place the potatoes in a strainer and press with the back of a spoon to remove all the moisture. In a medium bowl combine the potatoes, salt, pepper, garlic, thyme, vinegar, egg, and 2 tablespoons olive oil. Pat the mixture into a well-oiled 9-inch pie dish. Bake for 30 minutes. Remove from the oven and brush the crust with the remaining olive oil.

Arrange the tomatoes in concentric overlapping circles on the potatoes. Sprinkle with the cheese and basil. Season with salt and pepper to taste and return to the oven. Bake for 15 to 20 minutes until the cheese is light brown and bubbly. Remove and allow to cool for 5 minutes before cutting into wedges.

Serves 6

Southern Sunshine Spoon Bread

Real southern comfort that you can eat with a spoon. Serve with sautéed sausages or slabs of country ham.

1 cup minus 1 tablespoon
yellow cornmeal

3 cups milk

1 tablespoon unsalted butter

3 large eggs

$\frac{1}{2}$ teaspoon salt

1 tablespoon sugar

PLACE an oven rack in the lower third of the oven and preheat to 400°F. Butter a $1\frac{1}{2}$-quart soufflé or baking dish.

Stir the cornmeal and 2 cups of the milk together in a medium saucepan. Bring to a boil over medium heat and cook, stirring constantly, until the mixture is the thickness of mashed potatoes. Remove from the heat and stir in the remaining milk and the butter. In a small bowl, whisk the eggs with the salt, sugar, and baking powder. Whisk into the cornmeal mixture and pour into the prepared dish.

Bake for 30 minutes, until the top is golden brown and the spoon bread is firm when shaken gently. Serve drizzled with warm maple syrup.

Serves 4

New Mexican Roasted Potato Wedges

These ranch-style potato wedges are great with Huevos Ranchitos (page 20) or Scrambled Eggs and Pan-Seared Mushrooms and Peppers (page 11).

2 tablespoons olive oil

2 teaspoons chili powder

1 teaspoon ground cumin

1 teaspoon paprika

$\frac{1}{2}$ teaspoon salt

$\frac{1}{8}$ teaspoon coarsely ground
black pepper

2 large baking potatoes
($\frac{3}{4}$ pound each)

PLACE an oven rack in the lower third of the oven and preheat to 400°F.

In a medium bowl, mix together the oil, chili powder, cumin, paprika, salt, and pepper. Cut the potatoes in half lengthwise, then cut each half into long quarters. Toss with the oil mixture and place on a rimmed baking sheet, cut sides down. Drizzle any remaining oil over the wedges and bake for 10 minutes. Loosen the potatoes with a spatula and turn. Continue baking for a total of 30 minutes, or until the potatoes are very brown and crispy.

Serves 4

Stilton Rarebit and Oven-Roasted Tomatoes

This very British mixture of cheeses and beer, seasoned with a touch of mustard and pepper, is very soothing to your insides, both visceral and cerebral. Moist, chewy little crumpets are perfect for this sauce, but English muffins or even toast will do.

6 plum tomatoes, halved crosswise

1 tablespoon olive oil

Salt and coarsely ground black pepper to taste

$1/2$ cup dark beer

$1/2$ pound extra-sharp Cheddar cheese, grated

4 ounces Stilton cheese, crumbled

1 tablespoon all-purpose flour

1 large egg

1 teaspoon dry mustard

1 teaspoon Worcestershire sauce

$1/2$ teaspoon paprika

$1/8$ teaspoon white pepper

Pinch of cayenne

4 crumpets, English muffins, or toasts

To roast the tomatoes: Preheat the oven to 400°F.

In a small bowl, toss the tomatoes with the olive oil and salt and pepper. Place them, cut sides down, on a baking sheet and roast for 10 minutes. The skins will start to split, but the tomatoes will still be firm to the touch. Allow them to rest on the pan for 10 minutes while you make the rarebit.

In the top of a double boiler placed over simmering water, heat the beer. In a small bowl, combine the cheeses with the flour and slowly stir into the beer. Stir constantly until the cheeses melt. Stir in the egg and continue cooking and stirring until the mixture thickens slightly. Season the rarebit with the mustard, Worcestershire, paprika, white pepper, and cayenne. Spoon over toasted crumpets or English muffins.

Serves 4

Thin-Crusted Pizza

If leftover pizza is your idea of the perfect breakfast, then prepare this version in half the time it takes to make oatmeal. I make pizza toppings from all kinds of leftovers. Spread last night's vegetable dish or fruit dessert on a crisp golden tortilla and top with a sprinkling of cheese or drizzle with honey.

Two 8-inch flour tortillas

1 tablespoon olive oil

Topping Combinations

Vegetarian refried beans

Shredded cooked chicken

Diced green chilies

Grated Cheddar cheese

◆

Goat cheese

Roasted red or yellow bell
  peppers

Whole roasted garlic cloves

◆

Fresh tomato slices

Whole basil leaves

Grated mozzarella cheese

◆

Crumbled cooked Italian
  sausage

Crushed red pepper

Grated fontina cheese

◆

Caramelized onions

Roasted eggplant slices

Grated fontina cheese

◆

Thinly sliced ham

Thin red onion slices

Grated Jarlsberg cheese

◆

Lowfat ricotta cheese

Sliced peeled peaches

Honey

PLACE an oven rack in the center of the oven and preheat to 400°F.

Brush one side of each tortilla with olive oil and stack one on top of the other, oiled sides up, on a baking sheet. Bake for 5 minutes, until the bottom tortilla is light brown and the top tortilla begins to puff. Remove the tortillas from the oven and place the oven rack about 4 inches from the broiler. Turn on the broiler.

Arrange the topping on each tortilla and broil until the topping is bubbly and heated through. Remove them to a cutting board, let rest for 2 minutes, and cut into quarters.

Makes 2 pizzas

Turkey Hash

This recipe is based on the leftovers I typically have after Thanksgiving. Use your imagination here; don't be afraid to toss together a loose version of this from last night's dinner. I top this with a poached egg for breakfast or serve it with a green salad for lunch. If you do find a bit of leftover bread stuffing at some other time of year, this same recipe will work with ground turkey.

4 cups bread stuffing

3 cups cubed cooked turkey
(about ¾ pound)

1 cup peas and onions

½ cup whole-berry cranberry
sauce

½ cup diced Brussels sprouts
(optional)

1 cup chopped candied yams

¾ cup turkey or chicken broth

2 tablespoons safflower oil

IN a large bowl, combine the stuffing, turkey, peas and onions, cranberry sauce, Brussels sprouts, yams, and broth. Heat the oil in a 12-inch skillet over medium-high heat. Press the stuffing mixture into the bottom of the pan and cook until well browned. With a wide spatula, turn the hash to the other side and cook until lightly browned. Cut into wedges or break into chunks.

Serves 4

Turkey and Sage Sausage Patties

I*n the time it takes to thaw frozen sausage, you can make your own patties using whatever ingredients you choose. Preservative free and low in fat, these patties take advantage of widely available ground turkey. Cook the patties in a nonstick pan to reduce the fat even more.*

1 pound ground turkey

2 to 3 tablespoons
 safflower oil

2 cloves garlic, minced

1/2 teaspoon salt

1/4 teaspoon coarsely ground
 black pepper

1 tablespoon dried sage

1 tablespoon dried thyme

1/4 teaspoon cayenne

1/8 teaspoon ground allspice

1/2 teaspoon fennel seeds

PREHEAT the oven to 250°F.

In a medium bowl or a food processor fitted with the metal blade, combine the turkey, 2 tablespoons oil, the garlic, salt, pepper, sage, thyme, cayenne, allspice, and fennel seeds. Stir or pulse together until well mixed.

Heat a heavy sauté pan over medium heat and film with the remaining tablespoon of oil, or heat a nonstick pan without oil. Shape the turkey mixture into 2½-inch patties about ¼ inch thick. There should be about 10. Cook in batches until browned on both sides and the centers feel firm when pressed with a finger, about 5 minutes. Remove to an oven-proof platter to keep warm in the oven until all the sausages are cooked and ready to serve.

Makes 10 patties

Ham and Sweet Potato Hash

S*weet potatoes can replace others in most any recipe, but they give this hash a distinctly original flavor. Fill Thin and Crispy Cornmeal Crêpes (page 29) with this hash for a hearty breakfast.*

1 tablespoon safflower oil

3 tablespoons chicken broth

1½ pounds sweet potatoes or
 yams, diced with peel

1 small onion, diced

1 cup diced ham

Salt and coarsely ground black
 pepper to taste

IN a heavy 10-inch skillet over medium-high heat, heat the oil and broth. Add the sweet potatoes and cook until the liquid has evaporated and the potatoes are barely tender. Add the onion and the ham. Continue cooking over medium heat, stirring and scraping the bottom of the pan, until everything is browned and very tender, about 30 minutes. Season with salt and pepper and serve.

Serves 4

Spicy Oven-Roasted Bacon

It's hard to believe that crispy strips of smoky, salty bacon can be improved upon, but I think I've done it with a little brown sugar and spicy heat.

½ cup packed light brown
  sugar

2 tablespoons chili powder

1 teaspoon ground cumin

1 teaspoon cumin seeds

1 teaspoon ground coriander

¼ teaspoon cayenne

1 pound thick-sliced bacon
  (about 12 slices)

PLACE an oven rack in the center of the oven and preheat to 400°F. Line a rimmed 15- by 11½-inch baking pan with foil. Place a baking rack on the foil.

In a small bowl, combine the sugar, chili powder, ground cumin, cumin seeds, coriander, and cayenne. Spread mixture out on a piece of wax paper and form into a 12-inch square. Press each side of the bacon slices into the mixture to coat heavily. Lay the bacon strips, barely touching, on the rack over the foil.

Bake for 12 minutes. Turn the bacon over with tongs and continue baking for another 10 minutes, until the bacon looks deep brown but not burned. Remove from the oven and allow to cool on the rack for 10 minutes before serving.

Serves 4 to 6

Fresh Fig, Prosciutto, and Parmesan Sandwich

We are very lucky to have a fig farm about a mile from our house. The owners grow about 24 different varieties of figs, several that can be tucked into this sublime sandwich. I pass this quickly under the broiler just to warm the Parmesan.

1 thick slice of walnut, or toasted seeds and raisin, or seedless rye bread, toasted

Unsalted butter or olive oil

4 large Black Mission, Adriatic, or Brown Turkey figs, stem ends trimmed and halved

2 slices prosciutto

Parmigiano-Reggiano cheese, shaved into strips with a vegetable peeler

Coarsely ground black pepper

PLACE an oven rack 4 inches from the broiler unit and preheat the broiler.

Lightly spread the toast with butter or olive oil. Lay the figs, cut sides up, on the bread. Drape the prosciutto over the figs and top with strips of the cheese. Place under the broiler just to warm the cheese, if desired, and sprinkle with pepper.

Makes 1 open-faced sandwich

Variations

*

Omit the cheese and drizzle with a tablespoon of honey.

*

Omit the prosciutto. Cover the toast with leaves of arugula before adding figs and Parmesan. Drizzle with olive oil before broiling briefly.

Braised Chicken Livers with Pineapple and Canadian Bacon

Dress up this sweet, smoky dish for a lavish brunch buffet or dress it down with a little brown rice or Whole-Wheat Biscuits (page 105) for a Sunday night supper.

1 cup all-purpose flour

½ teaspoon ground allspice

¼ teaspoon ground cloves

¼ teaspoon ground nutmeg

½ teaspoon salt

¼ teaspoon coarsely ground black pepper

1 pound chicken livers, trimmed of fat

3 ounces Canadian bacon (3 slices), cut into ½-inch strips

3 tablespoons unsalted butter

½ large pineapple, peeled, cored, and cut into 1-inch cubes

3 tablespoons safflower oil

½ cup reduced-sodium chicken broth

½ cup sherry vinegar

2 tablespoons finely chopped flat-leaf parsley for garnish

IN a medium bowl or small brown paper bag, combine the flour, allspice, cloves, nutmeg, salt, and pepper. Toss the chicken livers into the flour mixture. Shake the bag or toss well in the bowl to thoroughly coat the livers. Set aside.

In a 12-inch nonstick skillet over high heat, lightly brown the Canadian bacon. Add 2 tablespoons of the butter and sauté the pineapple for about 3 minutes. Using a slotted spoon, remove the bacon and the pineapple to a plate. Melt the remaining butter in the oil in the same skillet. Add the chicken livers in a single layer and cook, turning often, until firm and crispy. Return the bacon and pineapple to the skillet and add the chicken broth and vinegar. Cover, reduce the heat to a simmer, and cook for about 10 minutes, just until the liquid thickens slightly. Stir to coat the livers with sauce, sprinkle with the parsley, and serve.

Serves 4

Bruschetta with Chopped Liver and Apples

*A*lthough this country pâté is hard to resist eating warm from the pan, the flavors will improve if it is stored, covered, in the refrigerator for 4 days. Pile it on rustic bread and serve with scrambled eggs for breakfast, or substitute dry sherry or Madeira wine for the apple juice for a hearty hors d'oeuvre.

Twelve 1/2-inch slices of French or Italian bread

1 clove garlic, peeled

1/4 cup extra-virgin olive oil

1/2 cup (1 stick) unsalted butter

1 medium onion, chopped

1 pound chicken livers

2 medium tart apples, unpeeled, cored and coarsely chopped

1/4 cup finely chopped flat-leaf parsley

1/2 cup apple juice

1/2 teaspoon salt

1/4 teaspoon coarsely ground black pepper

4 hard-cooked large eggs, coarsely chopped

Finely chopped fresh chives or scallions for garnish

*G*RILL or toast the bread on both sides until golden brown. Rub one side with the garlic, then brush with the olive oil.

In a 12-inch skillet over medium heat, melt the butter and sauté the onion and chicken livers just until the onion is softened and the livers change color. Add the apples, parsley, apple juice, salt, and pepper and cook until the liquid has reduced by half, about 30 minutes. Stir in the eggs. Transfer the mixture to a food processor fitted with the metal blade and pulse just until coarsely chopped. Do not puree. Spoon the mixture on the bread and sprinkle with the chives or scallions and serve. The liver and apples can be stored in the refrigerator for up to 6 days.

Makes about 2 cups

Salmonburgers

*P*erched atop English muffin halves and spread with a little mayonnaise thinned with lemon juice, Salmonburgers are *perfectly suited to easy entertaining. Alternatively, shape the mixture into 2-inch patties and serve with scrambled eggs.*

1 pound salmon fillets, skin removed and cut into ¼-inch dice

1 tablespoon Dijon mustard

1 teaspoon prepared horseradish

¼ teaspoon salt

¼ teaspoon coarsely ground black pepper

½ cup soft fresh bread crumbs

1 tablespoon olive oil

In a large bowl, toss the salmon with the mustard, horseradish, salt, pepper, and bread crumbs. Form into 4 patties about 2½ inches in diameter.

In a heavy, preferably nonstick skillet, heat the olive oil over medium-high heat. Add the burgers and cook until brown and crispy on the bottom, about 3 minutes. Turn and cook the other side.

Serves 4

Smoked Salmon Roll

K*eep flour tortillas on hand as you would bread and crackers. They're great for filling with just about anything— savory or sweet. This "sandwich" is perfect for breakfast on the run or sliced and served as an hors d'oeuvre.*

¼ cup lowfat or whipped cream cheese

1 tablespoon finely chopped fresh dill

Two 8- or 9-inch fresh flour tortillas, at room temperature

4 ounces smoked salmon, thinly sliced

¼ English cucumber, unpeeled, very thinly sliced

1 tablespoon capers, drained

1 cup alfalfa sprouts

In a small bowl, combine the cream cheese and dill. Spread the mixture evenly over one side of each tortilla. Arrange the salmon slices on one half of the cream cheese and top with the cucumber, capers, and sprouts. Beginning on the salmon side, roll the tortilla tightly and serve whole or slice into 4 to 6 rounds.

Makes 2 rolls

Crunchy Crab Cakes

Whether topped with a poached egg and salsa, sandwiched between toasted English muffins, or partnered with roasted red peppers and a mixed green salad, these crispy crab cakes are a snap to prepare.

1 pound shelled crabmeat

2 tablespoons finely chopped
   flat-leaf parsley

2 scallions, finely chopped

1 cup fresh bread crumbs

1 tablespoon Dijon mustard

2 tablespoons mayonnaise

1 tablespoon lemon juice

1 large egg, lightly beaten

Dash of Tabasco sauce

Salt and coarsely ground black
   pepper

2 tablespoons olive oil

In a medium bowl, stir together the crabmeat, parsley, scallions, and 1/2 cup of the bread crumbs. In a small bowl, stir together the mustard, mayonnaise, lemon juice, egg, and Tabasco. Stir into the crab mixture. Shape into 3-inch patties approximately 1/2 inch thick. The cakes may be prepared to this point and refrigerated, covered, overnight.

In a saucer or flat dish, spread the remaining bread crumbs and season with salt and pepper. Press each side of the crab cakes into the seasoned bread crumbs. Heat the oil in a heavy 10-inch skillet over high heat and cook the cakes until lightly browned on the bottom, about 3 minutes. With a wide spatula, turn the cakes and cook until browned on the opposite side. Serve immediately.

Serves 4

Sweet Oven "Fried" Flautas

*F*lautas, or "little flutes," are typically filled with shredded chicken or beef and deep-fried. I've improvised here, wrapping fresh flour tortillas around a fruity, smooth filling and baking them in a very hot oven. If you're in the mood for something more savory, try the creamy hot and spicy variation.

Four 7- or 8-inch fresh flour tortillas, halved, at room temperature

$^1/_2$ cup lowfat cream cheese, ricotta, or Yogurt Cheese (page 140)

$^1/_4$ cup raspberry jam or orange marmalade

1 tablespoon milk

1 tablespoon sugar

PLACE an oven rack in the center of the oven and preheat to 450°F.

About $^1/_2$ inch from the cut edge of each tortilla half, spread about 1 tablespoon of the cheese and top with about $^1/_2$ tablespoon of the jam. Roll up tightly, starting at the cut edge. Place, seam side down, on a lightly greased baking sheet. Brush each flauta with the milk and sprinkle with the sugar. Bake until golden brown, 12 to 15 minutes.

Makes 8 flautas

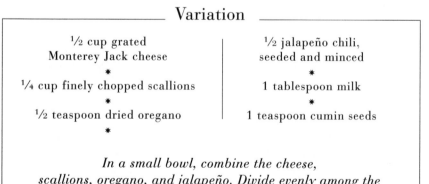

Variation

$^1/_2$ cup grated
Monterey Jack cheese

✱

$^1/_4$ cup finely chopped scallions

✱

$^1/_2$ teaspoon dried oregano

✱

$^1/_2$ jalapeño chili,
seeded and minced

✱

1 tablespoon milk

✱

1 teaspoon cumin seeds

In a small bowl, combine the cheese, scallions, oregano, and jalapeño. Divide evenly among the tortillas and roll them up tightly, starting at the cut edge. Place, seam side down, on a baking sheet. Brush each flauta with milk and sprinkle with the cumin seeds. Bake until golden brown, 12 to 15 minutes.

Cereals Hot and Cold

If your idea of cereal is limited to the boxed variety and an occasional bowl of oatmeal, chances are you haven't made your way out of the cereal aisle and into the local health food store or the bulk section of your supermarket. Brown rice, millet, kasha, quinoa, wheat berries, couscous, buckwheat—the possibilities go far beyond corn flakes, cream of wheat, and oatmeal. Best of all, a few ingredients can transform any one of these humble grains into a delicious, deeply satisfying meal. Bulgur seasoned with cinnamon, coriander, cloves, and orange zest and stirred together with dried fruit, pine nuts, and plain yogurt makes a wonderful Fruited Breakfast Tabbouleh (page 61). I like to make extra to have on hand for a light supper or side dish. A little maple syrup and milk are all you need to dress a soothing bowl of kasha, a wonderfully aromatic roasted buckwheat. ✳ As for cold cereal, taking the time to make your own allows you to create the flavors you want and to control what goes into the cereal bowl or in your hand, as the case may be. Among my favorites are Honey Apple Cinnamon Granola (page 57) and Multi-Grain, Multi-Seed, Multi-Nut Granola (page 58). I always have a supply of granola on hand for snacking or a quick topping for frozen yogurt, but I like it best in a bowl with cold milk. ✳ Use grains as breakfast building blocks. Keep a supply of honey, maple syrup, salt, cinnamon, dried fruits, milk, and yogurt on hand, and you can create satisfying breakfasts in a snap.

Dry-Roasted Oat and Almond Granola

This easy quick-cook method transforms simple ingredients into fragrant, toasty morsels clustered together with melted brown sugar. Allow the granola to cool before adding milk or yogurt to preserve the crunch.

1 cup old-fashioned oats

⅓ cup sliced unblanched
  almonds

⅓ cup wheat germ

¼ cup sunflower seeds

¼ cup shredded coconut

¼ cup firmly packed dark
  brown sugar

Pinch of salt

In a heavy 10-inch skillet over medium heat combine the oats and almonds. Stir constantly for 5 to 7 minutes, until they become golden and fragrant. Add the wheat germ, sunflower seeds, and coconut and continue stirring for 10 minutes. Add the brown sugar and salt and cook, stirring constantly, about 3 minutes more. Remove to a baking sheet to cool completely. Store the granola in an airtight container.

Makes about 2½ cups

Honey Apple Cinnamon Granola

Making granola at home allows you to create your own special blend of breakfast cereal. Oats sweetened with concentrated apple juice and a little honey revive the memory of an old-fashioned apple crisp dessert. Serve with slices of fresh summer fruit.

10 cups old-fashioned (*not* quick or instant) oats

1 cup nonfat milk powder

¹⁄₂ cup oat bran (optional)

One 12-ounce can frozen unsweetened apple juice concentrate, thawed

¹⁄₂ cup safflower oil

¹⁄₂ cup honey

¹⁄₂ teaspoon almond extract

¹⁄₂ teaspoon salt

3 tablespoons ground cinnamon

1 teaspoon ground cloves

2 cups dried apple slices, coarsely chopped

PLACE an oven rack in the center of the oven and preheat to 325°F. Line 2 rimmed baking sheets with parchment paper.

In a large bowl, combine the oats, milk powder, and oat bran, if using. In a small saucepan over low heat, combine the apple juice, oil, honey, almond extract, salt, cinnamon, and cloves and stir just until the honey is watery. Pour over the oat mixture and stir with a wooden spoon to combine evenly. Divide the mixture between the 2 pans and bake for 30 minutes, stirring once. Rotate the pans and continue baking for another 30 minutes. Remove and cool on the pans undisturbed. Add the apples and store in sealed plastic bags. The granola can be frozen.

Makes 12 cups

Multi-Grain, Multi-Seed, Multi-Nut Granola

If I were to package my own cereal, this would be it. Change the dry ingredients to accommodate your own tastes, but be sure to keep the proportions of wet to dry ingredients the same. This granola is full of clumps, making it very convenient to eat by the handful.

6 cups old-fashioned oats

1 cup rye flakes

1 cup wheat flakes

1 cup wheat bran

1 cup nonfat milk powder

1/2 cup raw wheat germ

1 cup raw sunflower seeds

1 cup raw pumpkin seeds (*pepitas*)

1 cup cashew pieces

1 cup sliced unblanched almonds

1 cup safflower oil

1 cup honey

1/2 cup barley malt syrup (available in health food stores)

1 tablespoon ground cinnamon

1 teaspoon salt

2 tablespoons vanilla extract

1/2 teaspoon almond extract

2 cups dried fruit, such as dark or golden raisins, cranberries, sour cherries, currants, diced apricots, apples, prunes, or a combination of any

PREHEAT the oven to 325°F. Line 2 rimmed baking pans with parchment paper.

In a large bowl, stir together the oats, rye flakes, wheat flakes, bran, milk powder, wheat germ, seeds, and nuts. In a small saucepan over low heat, stir together the oil, honey, malt syrup, cinnamon, salt, and vanilla and almond extracts until heated through, about 5 minutes. Add to the dry ingredients and stir to coat evenly.

Divide the granola between the 2 baking pans and bake for 20 minutes. Stir with a spatula, paying careful attention to the edges which cook faster, and rotate the pans. Bake for 20 minutes more, until lightly browned. Stir the granola again and bake for another 10 to 20 minutes, until uniformly golden brown. Remove and cool completely. Toss with the dried fruit and store in sealed plastic bags. The granola may be frozen.

Makes about 14 cups

Summer-Weight Granola

*R*eady-to-eat puffed cereals with oats
and nuts give this breakfast a lighter-than-air summertime feeling. When the
weather turns hot and humid, store the cereal in sealed plastic bags and use directly
from the freezer.

4 cups old-fashioned oats

2 cups puffed wheat

1 cup puffed rice

½ cup puffed millet
  (optional)

1 cup sesame seeds

1 cup sliced almonds

¾ cup safflower oil

½ cup honey

1 cup frozen unsweetened
  apple juice concentrate,
  thawed

2 teaspoons ground cinnamon

PREHEAT the oven to 350°F. Line 2 rimmed baking pans with parchment paper.

In a large bowl, combine the oats, puffed wheat, puffed rice, puffed millet, if using, sesame seeds, and almonds. In a small saucepan over low heat, combine the oil, honey, apple juice concentrate, and cinnamon and stir until heated through. Add to the dry mixture and stir to coat evenly.

Divide the granola evenly between the 2 baking pans and bake for 20 minutes. Shake the pan vigorously to move the granola around, or stir with a spatula, rotate the pans, and continue baking for another 20 minutes, until the granola is lightly browned.

Makes 10 cups

Cranberry Cinnamon Brown Rice Pudding

I *created this version of rice pudding because I love the flavor of tart cranberries and pungent, mildly sweet cinnamon. As creamy and rich as traditional rice pudding, it is lower in fat—a bonus! Use maple syrup in place of the honey if you like.*

½ cup brown rice

2 cups lowfat milk

½ teaspoon salt

1 tablespoon honey

½ teaspoon ground cinnamon

½ cup dried cranberries, raisins, or currants

Freshly grated nutmeg

IN a blender or food processor, grind the rice until the kernels are half their original size. Some will become powdered but some will remain almost whole.

In a medium saucepan over high heat, combine the rice, milk, salt, honey, cinnamon, and cranberries and bring to a boil. Cover, lower the heat, and simmer, stirring occasionally, until the mixture is thickened and very creamy, 15 to 20 minutes.

Serve in bowls with milk and a dusting of freshly grated nutmeg.

Serves 2

Fruited Breakfast Tabbouleh

Use the softest, best-quality dried fruit you can find for this sweet tabbouleh. Spoon it into a pita pocket, top with pine nuts and a dollop of yogurt, and breakfast (or lunch or dinner) is ready.

1 cup fine or medium bulgur

1½ cups boiling water

1 teaspoon salt

1 tablespoon sugar

1 teaspoon ground cinnamon

½ teaspoon ground coriander

⅛ teaspoon ground cloves

1½ teaspoons finely chopped orange zest

¼ cup orange juice

¼ cup safflower oil

2 cups diced mixed dried fruit, such as raisins, apricots, prunes, figs, apples, pears, cherries, or currants

¼ cup toasted pine nuts (optional)

½ plain lowfat yogurt (optional)

In a medium bowl, stir the bulgur and boiling water together and allow to stand for 1 hour, or until all the liquid is absorbed. Press through a strainer to make sure the bulgur is as dry as possible. Return the bulgur to the bowl and stir in the salt, sugar, cinnamon, coriander, cloves, and zest. Add the orange juice and oil and stir to combine. Add the fruit and stir. Sprinkle with the pine nuts and top with yogurt, if using, and serve. The tabbouleh can be refrigerated, covered, for up to 3 days.

Fills 4 pitas

Variations

Use any of the following in place of the fruit and nuts.

½ cup crumbled cooked bacon

*

½ cup pitted Kalamata olives

*

½ cup crumbled feta cheese

*

2 medium tomatoes, seeded and chopped

*

2 tablespoons toasted sesame seeds

*

¼ cup each minced red and green bell peppers

*

½ cup finely chopped dry Italian salami

Kasha

Also known as roasted buckwheat, kasha has a subtle toasted flavor and a chewy texture. It cooks quickly and is ready to eat in 15 minutes.

1/4 teaspoon salt

1/2 cup kasha

Maple syrup and milk

IN a medium saucepan over high heat, combine 2 1/2 cups of water with the salt and bring to a boil. Stir in the kasha. Lower the heat and cook, uncovered, stirring frequently, for about 10 minutes. Spoon into bowls and add maple syrup and milk to taste.

Serves 2

Hot Wheat-Berry Cereal

Whole wheat berries are available in health food stores. Buy the soft berries rather than the hard for quicker cooking. Stir a few tablespoons of wheat berries into other hot cereals for a layer of texture and wheat flavor.

1/4 teaspoon salt

1 cup soft wheat berries

Brown sugar and milk

IN a small saucepan over high heat, combine 3 cups of water with the salt and bring to a boil. Stir in the wheat berries. Lower the heat to a simmer and cook for 1 hour. Add more water if the berries become dry. When done, the berries will be plump and chewy. Combine with other cereals such as oatmeal or farina or serve with brown sugar and milk. This can be cooked 2 days before using and kept covered and refrigerated.

Serves 2

Quinoa

Hailed the supergrain for its high protein content, quinoa is quick cooking, delicious, and easy to digest. If you buy it in bulk, rinse it several times before cooking. A sprinkling of sugar, a splash of milk, and a sliced fresh peach are all you need to appreciate this ancient grain.

¼ teaspoon salt

½ cup quinoa

Sugar and milk

IN a small saucepan over high heat, combine 1½ cups of water and the salt and bring to a boil. Stir in the quinoa, lower the heat, and bring to a simmer. Cook for 12 to 15 minutes, until all of the granules have become translucent and the liquid is absorbed. Spoon into bowls and serve with sugar and milk.

Serves 2

Vegetable, Bean, and Grain Salads

If you can eat waffles for dinner, then why not eat salad for breakfast? This chapter, more than any other, redefines the first meal of the day. If the only salad you associate with breakfast is the medley of underripe melon served in coffee shops, then you're in for some eye-openers here. In some of the recipes, I've incorporated familiar breakfast foods, while in others I take advantage of the huge variety of vegetables, beans, and grains that are now available in most supermarkets. Of course, there are bacon and eggs, but here they are tossed with fresh spinach, olives, and tomato and dressed with a tangy vinaigrette in Bacon and Egg Salad (page 67). One of my favorite breakfast (and lunch and dinner) salads is Wild Rice Salad (page 69). Currants, red grapes, and a sweet soy dressing transform humble rice into a super comforting breakfast. ✻ Think of grains and beans as you might pancakes or pasta—as canvases for your culinary imagination. Curiously, we are among the few cultures that don't routinely eat rice, couscous, or any of their relatives first thing in the morning. While it may not come naturally to you, eating grains with greens and beans at breakfast gives you just the jump start you need for the day. And don't forget, any one of these recipes makes a super lunch or light supper.

Wild Mushroom, Walnut, and Watercress Salad

Nestle a poached egg on this salad for a late breakfast or serve with a good piece of country walnut bread for lunch. Use chanterelles, morels, or whatever wild mushrooms are available.

½ ounce dried cèpe or porcini mushrooms

1 tablespoon unsalted butter

½ pound fresh crimini or shiitake mushrooms, brushed clean (stems removed from shiitakes) and sliced into ⅛-inch strips

¼ pound white mushrooms, brushed clean and sliced into ⅛-inch strips

3 tablespoons walnut oil

1 tablespoon red wine vinegar

1 tablespoon finely chopped shallots

1 tablespoon finely chopped fresh tarragon or 1 teaspoon dried tarragon

¼ teaspoon salt

¼ teaspoon coarsely ground black pepper

2 bunches watercress, washed and stemmed

½ cup walnuts, lightly toasted

Parmigiano-Reggiano cheese shaved into strips with a vegetable peeler

Soak the dried mushrooms in 1 cup of boiling water for ½ hour. Drain and slice into strips. In a 12-inch skillet over medium-high heat, melt the butter. Add the fresh mushrooms and sauté until they are soft and all of the liquid has evaporated. Set aside.

In a small bowl, whisk together the walnut oil, vinegar, shallots, tarragon, salt, and pepper. In a large bowl, combine the watercress and all the mushrooms with the oil and vinegar mixture. Sprinkle with the walnuts and strips of cheese.

Serves 4

Bacon and Egg Salad

*If, heaven forbid, you miss breakfast,
reclaim it at lunch with this salad composed of breakfast ingredients.*

½ pound mixed baby salad greens such as mesclun or spinach

½ cup halved and pitted Kalamata olives

2 large ripe tomatoes, seeded and diced

4 slices bacon, cooked and crumbled

½ cup olive oil

3 tablespoons white wine vinegar

1 teaspoon Dijon mustard

¼ teaspoon salt

¼ teaspoon coarsely ground black pepper

4 large eggs

Clover or alfalfa sprouts for garnish

DIVIDE the salad greens among 4 plates. In a small bowl, gently toss together the olives, tomatoes, and bacon. In another small bowl, whisk together the oil, 2 tablespoons of the vinegar, the mustard, salt, and pepper.

Fill a 10-inch skillet with water, add the remaining tablespoon of vinegar, and bring to a gentle boil. Crack the eggs into the water and poach until the whites are opaque and the yolks are barely set, about 3 minutes. Remove from the water with a slotted spoon and place an egg on each of the prepared plates. Cover with the tomato mixture and drizzle with the vinaigrette. Top with sprouts. Serve immediately.

Serves 4

Breakfast Salad with French Toast Croutons

I *want it all. I want sweet, eggy French toast, I crave early-spring tender green beans, and I love the crunch of apples and walnuts. Well, they're all here, tossed in a vinaigrette sweetened with a little maple syrup.*

For the Croutons

4 large eggs

½ cup milk

1 teaspoon vanilla extract

⅓ cup all-purpose flour

½ teaspoon baking powder

6 slices of firm white bread, cut into 1½-inch cubes

4 tablespoons unsalted butter

For the Salad

½ pound tender green beans, cut into 1½-inch pieces

½ head butter lettuce, torn into bite-sized pieces

1½ large tart apples, peeled, cored, and cut into 1-inch dice

½ cup walnuts, lightly toasted

For the Vinaigrette

1 tablespoon sherry vinegar

¼ cup safflower oil

2 tablespoons maple syrup

¼ teaspoon salt

Pinch of coarsely ground black pepper

To make the croutons: In a small bowl, whisk together the eggs, milk, vanilla, flour, and baking powder. Add the bread cubes and toss to coat. Spread in a single layer in a shallow pan and let rest for 1 hour, or cover and refrigerate overnight.

Preheat the oven to 250°F.

In a 12-inch nonstick skillet over medium heat, melt 2 tablespoons of the butter and sauté half of the bread cubes on both sides until golden brown. Repeat with the remaining cubes. Place the bread in the oven while assembling the salad.

To assemble the salad: In a large pot of lightly salted boiling water, cook the beans for 5 to 7 minutes, until tender. Remove and refresh in cold water. Drain and set aside.

Meanwhile, in a small bowl, whisk together the ingredients for the vinaigrette.

In a large bowl, combine the lettuce, apples, beans, walnuts, and croutons. Toss with the vinaigrette and serve immediately.

Serves 4 to 6

Wild Rice Salad

Wild rice, like pasta, provides endless opportunities for being enhanced. Studded with currants and sweet red grapes, then tossed in a tangy dressing, this salad is super for breakfast or, with a few strips of grilled chicken or chunks of smoked trout, becomes lunch or dinner.

For the Dressing

1 small juice orange, zest reserved, peel and pith removed, halved and seeded

3 tablespoons honey

1 tablespoon soy sauce

1 tablespoon safflower oil

$\frac{1}{2}$ teaspoon dry mustard

$\frac{1}{4}$ teaspoon ground ginger

$\frac{1}{2}$ teaspoon salt

$\frac{1}{8}$ teaspoon coarsely ground black pepper

For the Salad

1 cup wild rice

$\frac{1}{2}$ teaspoon salt

$1\frac{1}{3}$ cups seedless red grapes, halved

2 teaspoons grated orange zest

$\frac{1}{2}$ cup currants

$\frac{1}{4}$ cup coarsely chopped flat-leaf parsley

To make the dressing: In the bowl of a food processor, combine the orange halves, honey, soy sauce, oil, mustard, ginger, salt, and pepper and pulse until smooth. Set aside.

To make the salad: In a medium saucepan, bring 3 cups of water to a boil, add the rice and salt and stir. Cover, reduce the heat to low, and cook for 1 hour, or until the liquid is absorbed and the rice is tender. Remove to a strainer, drain, and pour into a large bowl.

Pour about half of the dressing over the rice and toss to combine. Let cool to room temperature. Add the grapes, orange zest, currants, and parsley and enough additional dressing to moisten the salad. Serve at room temperature or chilled. This can be made 1 day ahead, covered, and refrigerated.

Serves 4

Berries and Spinach Salad

Use strawberries and raspberries for a summer version of this gorgeous salad and cooked cranberries in the cold months. Flavored oils and vinegars are showing up everywhere these days; look for walnut oil and raspberry vinegar in specialty shops and large supermarkets.

1 bunch fresh spinach,
  washed, stemmed, and torn
  into bite-sized pieces

½ cup walnut oil

¼ cup raspberry vinegar

¼ teaspoon coarsely ground
  black pepper

2 cups strawberries, hulled
  and halved

1 cup raspberries

3 ounces Danish blue cheese,
  crumbled

PLACE the spinach in a large salad bowl. In a small bowl, whisk together the oil, vinegar, and pepper. Pour on the spinach and toss to coat all of the leaves. Add the strawberries, raspberries, and cheese and gently toss again.

Serves 4

White Beans and Orecchiette with Peas and Prosciutto

This is one of those salads you wish was in your refrigerator all the time. If you can't find orecchiette pasta, use any tube-shaped pasta.

½ pound dried white beans (navy or cannellini), soaked overnight in water to cover

Salt

2 cloves garlic, peeled

1 bay leaf

1 sprig of fresh thyme

½ pound orecchiette ("little ears")

¼ cup extra-virgin olive oil

2 teaspoons dried sage

2 tablespoons fresh thyme leaves

¼ pound prosciutto, cut into ½-inch strips

1 cup green peas, blanched for 2 minutes in boiling water

½ cup finely diced red onion

Coarsely ground black pepper to taste

DRAIN the beans and place in a medium saucepan with water to cover, about 1 inch. Add 1 teaspoon of salt, the garlic, bay leaf, and thyme. Bring just to a simmer over medium heat and simmer for 45 to 50 minutes, just until the beans are tender but not mushy. Drain the beans and discard the garlic, bay leaf, and thyme.

Meanwhile, bring 4 quarts of water to a boil and add the orecchiette and 2 tablespoons of salt. Cook until the pasta is tender, 8 to 12 minutes. Drain.

In a large bowl, combine the beans and pasta with the olive oil, sage, and thyme. Fold in the prosciutto, peas, and onion and season with salt and pepper. Serve at room temperature or chilled. Shards of Parmesan cheese can also be added.

Serves 8 to 10

Egg Salad with Baby Potatoes and Asparagus

Whether packed in a pita for a picnic or piled atop a bed of watercress or tender lettuce leaves for brunch or lunch, this is a meal in itself. Use blanched spinach when asparagus is not in season.

2 pounds baby red potatoes, quartered

³/₄ pound pencil-thin asparagus, ends trimmed

¹/₄ cup finely chopped red onion

2 tablespoons chopped fresh chives

1 tablespoon chopped flat-leaf parsley

1 teaspoon chopped fresh thyme or ¹/₂ teaspoon dried thyme

¹/₂ cup plain lowfat yogurt

3 tablespoons olive oil

2 tablespoons lemon juice

¹/₂ teaspoon salt

¹/₄ teaspoon coarsely ground black pepper

4 hard-cooked large eggs, peeled and cut crosswise into ¹/₄-inch slices

4 strips cooked bacon, crumbled (optional)

2 ounces gorgonzola or blue cheese (optional)

Cook the potatoes in boiling salted water for 5 to 10 minutes, until tender when pierced with the tip of a knife. Drain and let cool. Blanch the asparagus in boiling water for 2 minutes. Cut into 1¹/₂-inch pieces.

In a small bowl, combine the onion, chives, parsley, thyme, yogurt, olive oil, lemon juice, salt, and pepper. In a large bowl, combine the potatoes, eggs, and asparagus. Pour the dressing over and gently toss until all of the ingredients are coated. Garnish with bacon and cheese if you wish.

Serves 4

Yeast Breads and Coffee Cakes

Few things evoke feelings of comfort and nostalgia as much as yeasty breads and coffee cakes. From the moment the yeast and warm water begin to bubble and foam, your kitchen is filled with irresistible aromas. No machine-baked bread and certainly nothing from the grocery store bake shop can give you the feeling of accomplishment that shaping dough into loaves can. The doughs in this chapter are very easy to work with and incorporate ingredients you're likely to have in your cupboard. ✸ Use the loaf breads to make impromptu sandwiches. Or toast slices and slather with your favorite jam. Pure and Simple Whole-Wheat Bread (page 86) spread with honey and yogurt cheese and topped with slices of fresh peaches makes a delicious breakfast. Walnut bread topped with a mound of chicken salad and leaves of arugula is the perfect lunch. Sugar-Lump Bread (page 77) can become the ultimate French toast since it is already sweet and flavored with cinnamon. Toasting any bread brings the sugars to the surface, intensifying the texture and taste of the grains. Pair lightly buttered Toasted Seeds and Raisin Bread (page 89) with slices of sautéed apples and sharp Cheddar cheese. Take it another step by topping with cottage cheese and toasted sunflower seeds. ✸ Most of the coffee cakes I've created can easily double as desserts or snacks.

Indulge in Pull-Apart Sugar and Spice Brioche (page 78) and a cup of lemony tea if you are craving a little something before bedtime. Make the dough for Overnight Cinnamon Twists (page 83) a day in advance and tuck one into a lunch bag in the morning. One of my favorite all-day "coffee cakes" is Whole-Wheat Cinnamon Roll Cupcakes (page 84). The dough can be made a day in advance, and the cleanup is a snap.

Chocolate Babka

Slather Yogurt Cheese (page 140) on this traditional Polish sweet yeast bread and wash it down with a perfect cup of French roast coffee. The dough must be prepared the day before you plan to bake the babka.

For the Dough

1 cup (2 sticks) unsalted butter

$1/2$ cup milk

$1/2$ cup sugar

1 tablespoon vanilla extract

Two $1/4$-ounce packages dry yeast

$1/4$ cup warm water (105° to 110°F.)

3 large eggs, at room temperature

3 cups all-purpose flour

$1/2$ cup unsweetened cocoa powder, preferably Dutch process

$1/2$ teaspoon salt

For the Filling

$1/2$ cup walnut pieces, lightly toasted

$7 1/2$ ounces almond paste

3 tablespoons unsalted butter

$1/2$ teaspoon almond extract

$1/2$ cup all-purpose flour

$1/3$ cup powdered sugar

$3/4$ cup dried sour cherries, dried cranberries, or raisins

$2/3$ cup semisweet chocolate chips

Powdered sugar for dusting

To make the dough: In a small saucepan over low heat, combine the butter, milk, and sugar and cook until the butter melts. Add the vanilla and set aside to cool to 100°F.

In a large mixing bowl, dissolve the yeast in the warm water and let stand for 5 minutes. Add the butter mixture, eggs, flour, cocoa, and salt and beat until smooth. Cover the bowl and refrigerate for at least 24 or up to 48 hours. The dough will double and have a cracked surface.

Lightly butter a 12-cup tube pan.

To make the filling: In a food processor fitted with the metal blade, grind the walnuts to a fine texture. Add the almond paste, butter, and almond extract and pulse until well combined. Add the flour and powdered sugar and pulse until the mixture forms coarse crumbs.

To make the babka: Turn the dough out onto a well-floured surface and divide into 2 equal pieces. Roll each piece into a 16- by 10-inch rectangle. Crumble half of the filling evenly over each piece. Sprinkle each with half of the cherries and half of the chocolate chips. Roll up, jelly-roll style, beginning at the long side. Place, seam side down, with the ends slightly overlapping, in the prepared pan. Repeat with the remaining dough and place the roll in the pan on top of the first roll. Cover the pan with a cloth and let rise in a warm place for 2 to 3 hours, until doubled.

Place an oven rack in the middle of the oven and preheat to 375°F.

Bake the babka for 45 to 50 minutes, until it is firm and dry on the top. Let cool completely in the pan. Gently invert onto a plate and dust with powdered sugar.

Serves 12

Sugar-Lump Bread

*Serve this bread as the Dutch do—
slathered with creamy unsalted butter alongside a cup of piping hot coffee.*

1 cup whole or lowfat milk

One ¼-ounce package dry
yeast

2 tablespoons sugar

½ cup (1 stick) unsalted
butter, softened

2 teaspoons salt

1 teaspoon finely chopped
lemon zest

5½ cups bread flour

2 tablespoons softened butter
for preparing pans

1½ cups sugar cubes

1½ tablespoons ground
cinnamon

1 egg yolk for glazing loaves

In a small saucepan, combine the milk with 1 cup of water and heat until warm to the touch (110°F.). Pour into the bowl of an electric mixer and stir in the yeast and sugar. Let the yeast proof until foamy, about 10 minutes. Add the butter, salt, and zest and beat on low speed until combined. The butter may not melt completely. Turn to medium speed and gradually add the flour, mixing until a soft, sticky dough is formed and the dough pulls away from the sides of the bowl. Using the dough hook, knead on medium speed for 10 minutes. Alternatively, turn out the dough onto a lightly floured surface and knead by hand, adding as little additional flour as necessary to prevent sticking, until the dough is smooth and elastic. Return the dough to a clean, lightly oiled bowl and let it rise, covered, until doubled, 1½ to 2 hours.

Place an oven rack in the center of the oven and preheat to 400°F. Using the 2 tablespoons of butter, grease 2 loaf pans measuring 8½" × 4½" × 2½".

Punch the dough down and divide in half. Cover lightly and allow to rest for 15 minutes. Place the sugar cubes in a plastic bag and crack with a small hammer or rolling pin. Pour into a small bowl and combine with the cinnamon. Roll each half of dough to a 16- by 8-inch rectangle. Sprinkle with half of the cinnamon-sugar mixture, distributing the sugar as evenly as possible. Beginning at one of the short sides, roll up as tightly as possible, jelly-roll style, tucking in the ends to seal. Place, seam side down, in the prepared pans, pressing on the dough to fill the corners. Cover loosely with plastic wrap and allow to double in volume, 1 to 1½ hours.

Brush the tops of the loaves with the egg yolk and bake for 40 to 45 minutes, until the loaves are a rich golden brown and sound hollow when tapped. Run a knife around the edges to loosen the loaves and turn them out onto a rack to cool completely before slicing.

Makes 2 loaves

Pull-Apart Sugar and Spice Brioche

If the name doesn't send you running into the kitchen, then the tantalizing aroma of this coffee cake will. For a holiday version, I stir in ¹/₂ cup of dried cranberries or dried sour cherries during the last few minutes of mixing the dough. This dough is easy to handle, but must be made with an electric mixer.

For the Dough

1 teaspoon dry yeast

2 tablespoons warm water
(105° to 110°F.)

2¹/₄ cups bread flour

2 tablespoons sugar

¹/₂ teaspoon salt

3 large eggs, at room
temperature

¹/₄ cup milk, at room
temperature

³/₄ cup (1¹/₂ sticks) cold
unsalted butter

For The Topping

³/₄ cup sugar

1¹/₂ teaspoons ground
cinnamon

¹/₄ teaspoon freshly grated
nutmeg

¹/₈ teaspoon ground cardamom

6 tablespoons unsalted butter

To make the dough: In a small bowl, sprinkle the yeast over the warm water and stir to dissolve. Add 3 tablespoons of the flour and a pinch of sugar and gently stir. Cover the bowl tightly with plastic wrap and let stand until doubled, 15 to 20 minutes.

In the bowl of an electric mixer fitted with a paddle attachment, combine the remaining flour, sugar, and salt. Add the eggs, milk, and yeast mixture and beat until well combined. With the mixer running, add the butter 1 tablespoon at a time, allowing each addition to become completely incorporated before adding another. Continue mixing until the dough looks smooth and elastic, about 5 minutes. The dough will not clean sides of bowl. Cover the bowl tightly with plastic wrap and allow to rise at room temperature for 2¹/₂ to 3 hours, until doubled.

Stir the dough down, press the plastic wrap directly on top, cover the bowl tightly with plastic wrap, and refrigerate for at least 12 hours or as long as 3 days.

To make the topping: In a small bowl, stir together the sugar, cinnamon, nutmeg, and cardamom. Melt the butter over low heat and set aside.

To make the brioche: Butter an 8-inch springform pan. Remove the plastic wrap and place the dough on a well-floured surface. Divide in half and shape each half into 12 walnut-sized balls. Dip each ball into the melted butter and then roll in the sugar mixture, covering all sides. Place the balls 1 inch apart in staggered layers in the prepared pan. Sprinkle with 2 tablespoons of the remaining sugar mixture. Cover with plastic wrap and allow to double at room temperature, about 3 hours.

Place an oven rack in the center of the oven and preheat to 375°F.

Remove the plastic wrap from the pan and bake the brioche for 35 minutes, until it looks browned and crisp on top. Cool completely before removing the sides of the pan.

Serves 6

Swedish Almond Pâte à Chou Coffee Cake

This originated from the Swedish family of one of my dearest friends. I have adapted it only slightly. It is subtly sweet, a perfect accompaniment for afternoon tea or just right for a late Sunday breakfast.

For the Pastry

1 cup all-purpose flour

¼ teaspoon salt

½ cup (1 stick) cold unsalted butter

2 tablespoons ice water

¼ teaspoon almond extract

½ cup apricot jam

For the Topping

½ cup (1 stick) unsalted butter

¼ teaspoon salt

1 cup all-purpose flour

4 large eggs

1 teaspoon almond extract

For the Frosting

½ cup sliced almonds, lightly toasted

1½ cups powdered sugar

1 tablespoon lemon juice

½ teaspoon almond extract

3 tablespoons milk or cream

PLACE an oven rack in the lower third of the oven and preheat to 375°F.

To make the pastry: In the bowl of a food processor fitted with a metal blade, pulse the flour and salt together. Cut the butter into the flour and pulse until the mixture resembles coarse crumbs. Add the ice water and almond extract and process until the mixture forms a ball. The pastry can be refrigerated for 2 days, wrapped tightly in plastic wrap, or used immediately. Bring to room temperature before shaping.

Divide the dough in half and, with floured hands, press each piece out to a 10- by 4-inch rectangle 2 inches apart on a heavy baking sheet. Spread the apricot jam to within ½ inch of the edges of each rectangle. Set aside.

To make the pâte à chou topping: In a medium saucepan, bring 1 cup of water, butter, and salt to a boil. Quickly stir in the flour and beat with a wooden spoon until the dough leaves the sides of the pan and forms a ball. Remove from the heat and let cool for 5 minutes. Add the eggs, one at a time, beating vigorously after each addition, until the dough is smooth. Stir in the extract.

Spread half of the pâte à chou on each of the pastry rectangles and bake for 1 hour, until the topping looks puffed, golden brown, and dry. Remove from the oven and place the baking sheet on a rack to cool. With a spatula, slide each cake onto a serving dish.

To make the frosting: Preheat the oven to 350°F. Spread the almonds on a baking sheet and toast for 10 minutes, until fragrant. In a small mixing bowl, combine the powdered sugar, lemon juice, almond extract, and just enough of the milk to make a spreadable consistency. Spread the frosting evenly over both cakes, sprinkle with toasted almonds, and serve. This is best eaten the same day.

Makes 2 coffee cakes, each serving 6

Blackberry Breakfast Crumb Cake

Use the sweetest, freshest blackberries you can find. I don't like to substitute other berries in this cake because I look forward to the uniquely stained batter and light crunch of these wild fruits.

For the Crumb Topping

⅓ cup all-purpose flour

¾ cup packed light brown sugar

1 cup coarsely chopped walnuts

2 teaspoons ground cinnamon

4 tablespoons unsalted butter, melted

For the Cake

½ cup (1 stick) unsalted butter

¾ cup granulated sugar

1 large egg

1 cup plain lowfat yogurt

1½ cups all-purpose flour

½ cup whole-wheat flour

1 teaspoon baking soda

1 teaspoon baking powder

½ teaspoon salt

1 teaspoon ground cinnamon

2 cups fresh blackberries

PLACE an oven rack in the center of the oven and preheat to 375°F. Lightly butter a 9-inch square baking pan.

To make the crumb topping: In a small bowl, combine the flour, brown sugar, walnuts, cinnamon, and butter. Set aside.

To make the cake: In a large bowl, cream the butter and sugar until light and fluffy. Add the egg and yogurt and beat until well combined. In another bowl, stir the flours, baking soda, baking powder, salt, and cinnamon together and add to the butter mixture. Mix until just blended.

Spread the batter over the bottom of the pan. Sprinkle evenly with the blackberries and cover with the topping. Bake for 40 to 45 minutes, until the edges are light brown and a toothpick inserted into the center of the cake comes out clean. Cool for 20 minutes before cutting.

Serves 9

Overnight Cinnamon Twists

This is a simple, rich dough—very easy to handle. It can be made in advance and shaped on the morning you want to serve the twists.

One ¼-ounce package dry
    yeast

¼ cup warm water (105° to
    110°F.)

4 cups all-purpose flour

1 cup (2 sticks) unsalted
    butter, at room temperature

1 cup sour cream or plain
    lowfat yogurt

2 large eggs, lightly beaten

1 teaspoon salt

1 teaspoon vanilla extract

1 cup sugar

2 teaspoons ground cinnamon

4 tablespoons (½ stick)
    unsalted butter, melted

In a small bowl, stir the yeast into the water until dissolved. Allow to stand until the liquid appears creamy, about 5 minutes.

In an electric mixer with the paddle attachment or in a large mixing bowl with a wooden spoon, combine the flour, butter, sour cream, eggs, salt, and vanilla. Stir in the yeast mixture and work until the dough is smooth. Cover the dough lightly with a damp cloth and plastic wrap and refrigerate for at least 2 hours or up to 2 days.

Place an oven rack in the center of the oven and preheat to 375°F. Line 2 baking sheets with parchment paper.

In a small bowl, combine the sugar and cinnamon. Remove the dough from the refrigerator and roll on a lightly floured surface into an 18- by 15-inch rectangle. Brush with some of the melted butter and sprinkle with one-quarter of the cinnamon-sugar mixture. Fold the short ends to meet in the center, fold in half along the seam, and give the dough a quarter turn. With the shorter ends parallel to your body, roll out again to an 18- by 15-inch rectangle, brush with melted butter, and sprinkle with one quarter of the cinnamon-sugar mixture. Repeat the procedure again. Roll out a fourth time to an 18- by 15-inch rectangle, brush with the remaining melted butter and sprinkle with the remaining sugar and cinnamon. Cut the dough lengthwise into 1-inch-wide strips, twist each strip by holding the ends and turning in opposite directions, and place 1½ inches apart on the baking sheets.

Bake for 20 minutes, until golden brown. Remove to a wire rack to cool.

Makes 15 to 18 twists

Whole-Wheat Cinnamon Roll Cupcakes

*B*aking a traditional cinnamon roll in *paper-lined muffin cups not only makes cleanup easier but allows you to eat one while driving! Since the dough can be prepared and refrigerated overnight, there is no excuse not to have freshly baked warm rolls in the morning.*

One $\frac{1}{4}$-ounce package dry
  yeast

1 tablespoon sugar

$\frac{1}{2}$ cup warm water (105° to
  110°F.)

3 tablespoons unsalted butter

2 tablespoons honey

$\frac{1}{2}$ cup milk

$1\frac{1}{4}$ teaspoons salt

1 large egg

2 cups whole-wheat flour

1 to $1\frac{1}{4}$ cups all-purpose
  flour

2 tablespoons unsalted butter,
  melted

$\frac{1}{2}$ cup packed light brown
  sugar

2 teaspoons ground cinnamon

$\frac{1}{2}$ cup raisins

For the Glaze

1 tablespoon unsalted butter,
  melted

1 tablespoon milk

2 teaspoons vanilla extract

1 cup powdered sugar

IN a large bowl, stir the yeast and sugar into the warm water. Allow to stand until foamy, about 5 minutes. Melt the butter and stir in the honey, milk, and salt. Stir into the yeast mixture along with the egg. Add the whole-wheat flour and enough of the all-purpose flour to make a soft dough. Turn out onto a well-floured surface and knead the dough for 8 to 10 minutes, using as much of the remaining flour as needed to prevent sticking. Form the dough into a ball and place it in an oiled bowl, turning to grease the top of the dough. Cover the bowl tightly with plastic wrap and allow the dough to rise in a warm, draft-free place for $1\frac{1}{2}$ to 2 hours, until doubled. Alternatively, allow the dough to rise, covered, in the refrigerator overnight.

Place an oven rack in the center of the oven and preheat to 400°F. Place paper liners in 10 muffin cups.

Turn the dough out onto a lightly floured surface and roll it into an 18- by 9-inch rectangle. Brush it with the melted butter. In a small bowl, combine the brown sugar and cinnamon and sprinkle it evenly over the dough. Sprinkle the raisins over the cinnamon mixture. Beginning at a long side, roll the dough tightly, jelly-roll style, tucking in the ends. Cut the dough into 10 equal pieces and place, cut sides up, in the muffin cups. Allow to rise, covered loosely with plastic wrap, for 45 minutes, until almost doubled. Bake for 18 to 20 minutes, until lightly browned. Remove the rolls from the muffin cups to a rack placed over wax paper.

To prepare the glaze: In a medium bowl, stir together the butter, milk, and vanilla. Stir in the powdered sugar to make a pourable consistency. The glaze should be the thickness of pancake batter. Spoon the glaze slowly over the warm rolls.

Makes 10 large rolls

Pure and Simple Whole-Wheat Bread

This large, earthy, fine-textured loaf will fill your kitchen with a seductive aroma. Thin slices make excellent toast. Thick slices make superb sandwich bread. Select the finest-quality stone-ground whole-wheat flour. With so few ingredients it's essential each be the best.

One ¼-ounce package dry yeast

2 cups warm water (105° to 110°F.)

2 tablespoons dark molasses

½ cup safflower oil

4 to 5 cups stone-ground whole-wheat flour

1½ teaspoons coarse salt

IN the bowl of an electric mixer or a large mixing bowl, sprinkle the yeast over the water. Allow to stand until foamy, about 5 minutes. Stir in the molasses and oil. Using the mixer's paddle attachment or a wooden spoon, beat in the flour until the dough pulls away from the sides of the bowl. Let the dough rest for 15 minutes, add the salt, and beat to incorporate. Turn the dough out onto a floured surface or attach the dough hook to the mixer and knead until no longer sticky, 8 to 10 minutes. Form the dough into a ball and place it in an oiled bowl, turning to grease the top of the dough. Cover the bowl tightly with plastic wrap and allow the dough to rise in a warm, draft-free place until doubled, about 1 hour. Check to see if the dough is ready by pressing the top with your finger. If the dent remains, the dough has risen enough.

Place an oven rack in the center of the oven and preheat to 375°F. Butter a loaf pan measuring 9" × 5" × 3½".

Punch the dough down and roll into a 16- by 9-inch rectangle. Beginning at a short side, tightly roll the dough up, jelly-roll style, tucking in the ends, and place seam side down in the pan. Press on the dough with your knuckles to push into the corners of the pan and flatten the top. Loosely cover the pan with plastic wrap and allow the dough to rise until doubled. It will rise above the rim of the pan. Bake for 1 hour, until the top is well browned and the bread sounds hollow when tapped on top. Turn the bread out onto a rack to cool completely before slicing.

Makes 1 large loaf

Walnut Bread

A *slice of this bread toasted and spread with a little fresh goat cheese is heavenly. I serve it with practically everything— from rich winter soups to light summer salads. Find barley malt in natural and health food stores. Note that the dough is started the night before.*

For the Sponge

1 cup warm water (105° to 110°F.)

One ¼-ounce package dry yeast

1 tablespoon nonfat dry milk

1 cup whole-wheat flour, preferably stone-ground

For the Dough

1½ cups warm water (105° to 110°F.)

2 tablespoons barley malt syrup

2 cups white bread flour, plus additional for kneading and shaping

⅓ cup nonfat dry milk

3 tablespoons walnut oil

2 cups whole-wheat flour

3 cups walnuts, lightly toasted

To make the sponge: In a large bowl, combine the water and yeast and allow to stand until foamy, about 5 minutes. With a wooden spoon, stir in the dry milk and flour. The mixture will be sticky. Cover the bowl tightly with plastic wrap and leave in a warm place (70° to 74°F.) overnight or at least for 8 hours.

To make the dough: Stir the water, malt syrup, and bread flour into the sponge. The dough will have some small lumps. Cover tightly with plastic wrap and leave in a warm place for 4 hours. The dough will be covered with small bubbles and will have risen and fallen. If using an electric mixer, attach the dough hook or stir with a wooden spoon and work the dry milk, oil, and whole-wheat flour into the dough. Continue kneading for 10 minutes; the dough will *not* pull away from the sides of the bowl. Alternatively, lightly flour your work surface and hands and using a dough scraper, knead the dough until it feels smooth and elastic. Add just enough of the bread flour to prevent sticking. Return the dough to a clean oiled bowl, cover with plastic wrap, and allow to rise until doubled, about 1 hour. Turn the dough out onto a lightly floured surface and allow to rest for 5 minutes. Meanwhile, butter a 9" × 5" × 3½" loaf pan.

Pat the dough out into a 12-inch square and spread half of the walnuts over the top. Carefully knead the dough until the walnuts have been incorporated, then add the remaining walnuts. Some of the nuts will work through the dough, but push them back in. When all the nuts are kneaded in, press the dough out into a 9-inch square. Fold the dough in half, seal the edges with the heel of your hand, and tuck in the ends. Place in the loaf pan, pressing with your knuckles to fill all the corners. Cover the pan loosely with plastic wrap and allow the dough to rise until it has come just above the rim of the pan, about 50 minutes.

Place an oven rack in the lower third of the oven and preheat to 400°F.

With a single-edged razor blade or very sharp knife, make 3 arched cuts, each about $1/2$ inch deep, on top of the dough. Bake for 50 to 60 minutes, until the top is browned and the bread sounds hollow when tapped on top. Remove from the pan and cool completely before slicing.

Makes 1 large loaf

Toasted Seeds and Raisin Bread

*L*oaded with crunchy seeds and sweet *raisins and molasses, this bread makes wonderful toast. Slather it with a little Yogurt Cheese (page 140), top with sliced bananas, and drizzle with honey for delicious take-along open-faced sandwiches.*

1 cup raw sunflower seeds

1/4 cup sesame seeds

1/4 flaxseed (available in health-food stores)

2 cups black raisins

1 cup golden raisins

One 1/4-ounce package dry yeast

1/2 cup warm water (105° to 110°F.)

1/2 cup molasses

1 1/4 cups water

1/2 cup nonfat dry milk

4 1/2 cups whole-wheat flour

2 teaspoons salt

3 tablespoons safflower oil

1 cup all-purpose flour

P\REHEAT the oven to 350°F.

Spread the seeds out on a baking sheet and toast for 15 minutes until lightly browned. Remove and cool to room temperature. Plump the raisins in hot water to cover for 30 minutes and drain. Meanwhile make the sponge. In a large bowl, sprinkle the yeast over the warm water and allow to stand 5 minutes until foamy. Add the molasses, water, and the dry milk and stir with a wooden spoon until blended. Add 2 cups of the whole-wheat flour and stir until a thick batter is formed. Cover the bowl tightly with plastic wrap and leave at room temperature until the sponge doubles and small bubbles appear on the top, 3 to 4 hours.

With the paddle attachment of a mixer or with a wooden spoon, beat in the salt, oil, the remaining whole-wheat flour, all-purpose flour, seeds, and raisins. Mix until a stiff dough forms. Change to the dough hook, or turn out onto a floured surface, and knead until the dough is smooth, about 10 minutes. Form into a ball and return to the bowl. Cover tightly with plastic wrap and allow the dough to double, about 2 hours.

Place an oven rack in the center of the oven and preheat to 375°F. Generously oil a 9 1/2" × 5" × 2 3/4" bread pan. Punch down the dough, knead a few times to expel any air, and shape into 1 large loaf. Place in the prepared pan. Cover loosely with plastic wrap and allow the dough to rise until it comes just over the top of the pan, 1 1/2 to 2 hours.

Bake in the center of the oven for 55 to 60 minutes, until the top is well browned and sounds hollow when tapped. Turn the bread out onto a rack to cool completely before slicing.

Makes 1 large loaf

Yeasted Buttermilk Corn Bread

The sheer size of this corn bread is impressive, but no more than its perfect crumb and wonderful aroma. It is great for toasting or sandwich-making and also makes wonderful croutons.

One ¼-ounce package dry yeast

¼ cup warm water (105° to 110°F.)

2 cups buttermilk

⅓ cup honey

5 tablespoons unsalted butter, at room temperature

2½ teaspoons salt

7¼ cups all-purpose flour

1 cup yellow cornmeal

½ teaspoon dry mustard

2 large eggs, well beaten

1 egg white, slightly beaten

1 tablespoon sesame seeds

IN a small bowl, sprinkle the yeast over the warm water and allow to stand until foamy, about 5 minutes. In a small saucepan over low heat, heat the buttermilk, honey, butter, and salt until the mixture is 110°F. The butter does not have to melt. Set aside.

In the bowl of an electric mixer fitted with the paddle attachment, combine the buttermilk mixture and 3 cups of the flour. With the mixer running, add the dissolved yeast, cornmeal, mustard, and eggs. Continue to mix on medium speed until thoroughly combined. Gradually add 4 more cups of the flour until a stiff dough is formed. Change to the dough hook or turn the dough out onto a well-floured surface and knead in the remaining ¼ cup flour. Continue to knead for 10 minutes, until the dough is smooth and elastic and pulls away from the sides of the bowl. Form the dough into a ball and place it in an oiled bowl, turning to grease the top of the dough. Cover the bowl tightly and allow the dough to rise in a warm draft-free place for 1½ to 2 hours, until doubled.

Place an oven rack in the center of the oven and preheat to 375°F. Generously grease a 9½" × 5" × 2¾" loaf pan.

Turn the dough out onto a floured surface and knead for a minute or two. Shape by flattening the dough into a 9- by 9-inch square. Fold one side into the center, then the opposite side over the fold and seal. Roll gently with the palms of your hands to form a cylinder, tucking in the ends. Place the dough, seam side down, in the loaf pan. Allow to rise in a warm place, uncovered, for 1 hour, until the dough rises slightly above the rim of the pan. Brush the top with beaten egg white and sprinkle with sesame seeds. Bake for 55 to 60 minutes, until the loaf rises at least 3 inches above the rim of the pan and is golden brown. Turn out on its side onto a cooling rack. Allow to cool completely before slicing.

Makes 1 large loaf

Olive and Pepper Focaccia

Think of this soft, thick, and chewy focaccia as your toast for breakfast, sandwich bread for lunch, and bread for dinner. Or top it with cheese and coarsely chopped sun-dried tomatoes and you have an impromptu pizza.

2 large baking potatoes, peeled and cut into 2-inch chunks

Two ¼-ounce packages dry yeast

1 teaspoon sugar

3 to 3½ cups bread flour

3 teaspoons coarse salt

⅓ cup plus 3 tablespoons extra-virgin olive oil

1 teaspoon dried thyme or 2 teaspoons chopped fresh thyme

2 teaspoons dried rosemary or 1 tablespoon chopped fresh rosemary

1 tablespoon coarsely ground black pepper

1 cup Kalamata olives, pitted

½ cup grated imported Parmigiano-Reggiano cheese

Fresh rosemary for garnish (optional)

PLACE the potatoes in a medium saucepan with 2 cups of water and cook over medium-high heat for 20 to 25 minutes, until tender. Drain the potatoes, reserving 1 cup of the cooking water. Mash the potatoes while still hot and measure out 2 cups. Pour the reserved potato water into a small bowl and cool to 110°F. Stir the yeast and sugar into the potato water and allow to stand until foamy, about 5 minutes. Combine 3 cups of the flour, the mashed potatoes, 2 teaspoons of the salt, and 3 tablespoons of the olive oil in a large mixing bowl. Add the yeast mixture and beat until blended. Attach dough hook if using a standing mixer, or turn dough out onto a floured surface and knead by hand, adding enough of the remaining flour to make a smooth and elastic dough, about 10 minutes. Form dough into a ball and place in an oiled bowl, turning to coat the top surface. Cover the bowl with plastic wrap and allow the dough to rise at a cool room temperature until doubled in bulk, 1½ to 2 hours.

Place a baking stone or tile on the bottom rack of the oven and preheat to 500°F. Generously grease a 15- by 11-inch jelly-roll pan.

continued

In a small bowl, combine the remaining teaspoon of salt, the thyme, rosemary, pepper, and $^1/_3$ cup olive oil. Punch the dough down and press evenly into the jelly-roll pan. Allow to rise again, covered loosely with plastic wrap, in a cool place for 1 to $1^1/_2$ hours. Brush the bread with the herbed oil. Distribute the olives evenly over the surface and press deeply into the dough. Dimple the dough by pressing your fingers through it to the bottom of the pan. Sprinkle with the cheese and insert the sprigs of rosemary, if using.

Bake on the preheated stone for about 15 minutes, lower the heat to 375°F., and continue baking for 15 to 20 minutes, until the top is golden. Cut into squares and serve warm or at room temperature.

Makes 12 servings

Muffins, Scones, Quick Breads, and Doughnuts

The breads in this chapter do not depend on yeast. For the most part, they can be ready to eat in less than an hour. Muffins satisfy a craving for something sweet and are nutritious take-along breakfasts. If the thought of baking on a busy weekday morning sends you dashing to the cereal cupboard, look before you run at the recipe for Meal-in-a-Muffin, page 94. Make the batter the night before and slide the muffins into the oven to bake while you shower and dress. ✳ You can bake spontaneously if you stock your pantry and refrigerator with a few basic ingredients: all-purpose flour, whole-wheat flour, cornmeal, molasses, honey, unsweetened applesauce, old-fashioned oats, plain lowfat yogurt, buttermilk, and eggs. With these on hand, you have little excuse not to have hot muffins or biscuits for breakfast. Of course, incorporate your favorite morning foods into other meals. Why not have a Blueberry Buttermilk Muffin (page 97) with a chicken salad for lunch or a Chili Corn Bread Muffin (page 103) with fajitas for dinner?

Meal-in-a-Muffin

Perfect for grabbing on the way out the door, this soft, moist, muffin is packed with good-for-you ingredients. Stir the batter together the night before or even two days before baking, and you'll have warm muffins from the oven in 30 minutes.

1 cup unprocessed
 (miller's) bran

½ cup raw wheat germ

½ cup nonfat milk powder

1 cup all-purpose flour

1 tablespoon baking powder

1 tablespoon ground cinnamon

1½ cups grated carrots
 (2 large)

2 large eggs

½ cup unsweetened
 applesauce

½ cup molasses

½ cup safflower oil

⅓ cup skim or lowfat milk

½ cup raisins

PLACE an oven rack in the center of the oven and preheat to 400°F. Line 8 cups in a muffin pan with paper liners or grease well.

In a large bowl, combine the bran, wheat germ, milk powder, flour, baking powder, cinnamon, and carrots. In a small bowl, whisk together the eggs, applesauce, molasses, oil, and milk. Add the wet ingredients to the dry ingredients and stir just until moistened. Fold in the raisins. The batter can be covered with plastic wrap and refrigerated up to 2 days.

Spoon the batter in the muffin cups, mounding the tops. Bake for 20 to 25 minutes, until the tops are browned and crisp and the centers are firm when lightly pressed with a finger. Cool in the pan for 10 minutes before removing to a wire rack.

Makes 8 large muffins

Ginger Bran Muffins

Bran muffins are great, but ginger-infused bran muffins are sublime. I prefer fewer larger muffins, but you can stretch this recipe to make 10 medium-sized ones. All the complex tastes of gingerbread are in these muffins.

1½ cups unprocessed (miller's) bran

½ cup dark molasses

1 cup buttermilk

½ cup safflower oil

2 large eggs, lightly beaten

1 cup all-purpose flour

½ cup whole-wheat flour

2 teaspoons baking powder

½ teaspoon baking soda

2 teaspoons ground ginger

1½ teaspoons ground cinnamon

½ teaspoon ground allspice

½ teaspoon salt

½ cup raisins or currants

PLACE an oven rack in the center of the oven and preheat to 375°F. Line 8 to 10 muffin cups with paper liners or grease well.

In a medium bowl, stir together the bran, molasses, buttermilk, oil, and eggs. To allow the bran to absorb the liquids, let stand 20 minutes or cover and refrigerate overnight.

In a large bowl, combine the flours, baking powder, baking soda, ginger, cinnamon, allspice, and salt. Stir the bran mixture into the flour mixture just until moistened. Fold in the raisins.

Spoon the batter into the muffin cups, filling just to the rim for medium muffins and mounding the batter for large muffins. Bake for 20 to 25 minutes, until the centers are firm when lightly pressed with a finger, and a toothpick inserted in the center of a muffin comes out clean. Remove from the oven and allow to cool for 10 minutes in the pan before removing to a wire rack.

Makes 8 large or 10 medium muffins

Banana Bran Muffins

These are the next best thing to cupcakes—a perfect after-school treat or midnight snack.

1 cup whole-wheat flour

1 cup unprocessed (miller's) bran

1 tablespoon baking powder

¼ teaspoon salt

¾ cup packed dark brown sugar

1¼ cups mashed very ripe bananas (about 3 medium)

½ cup safflower oil

2 large eggs

1 teaspoon vanilla extract

½ cup currants or raisins

PLACE an oven rack in the center of the oven and preheat to 400°F. Line 8 muffin cups with paper liners or grease well.

In a medium bowl, stir together the flour, bran, baking powder, salt, and brown sugar. In another bowl, whisk together the bananas, oil, eggs, and vanilla. Stir the egg mixture gently into the dry ingredients just until moistened. Fold in the currants.

Spoon the batter into the muffin cups and bake for 25 minutes, until the centers are firm and a toothpick inserted in the center of a muffin comes out clean. Remove from the oven and cool in the pan for 10 minutes before removing to a wire rack.

Makes 8 large muffins

Maple Cornmeal Muffins with Dried Blueberries

Dried blueberries have an intense, true flavor and are becoming more widely available. Using them in muffins allows you to enjoy their sweet summer flavor anytime.

¾ cup cornmeal, yellow or white

1½ cups all-purpose flour

2 teaspoons baking powder

1 teaspoon baking soda

¼ teaspoon salt

1 large egg

⅓ cup pure maple syrup

1 cup buttermilk

4 tablespoons unsalted butter, melted

½ cup dried blueberries

Granulated sugar

PLACE an oven rack in the center of the oven and preheat to 400°F. Line 8 large muffin cups with paper liners or grease well.

In a medium bowl, stir together the cornmeal, flour, baking powder, baking soda, and salt. In another bowl, whisk together the egg, maple syrup, buttermilk, and butter. Stir into the dry ingredients until just combined, then fold in the blueberries.

Spoon the batter into the muffin cups, mounding the tops. Lightly sprinkle the tops with granulated sugar. Bake for 18 to 20 minutes, until the centers are firm to the touch when lightly pressed with a finger and the edges are golden brown. Remove from the oven and cool in the pan for 10 minutes before removing to a wire rack.

Makes 8 large muffins

Blueberry Buttermilk Muffins

This recipe has been in my recipe file for more than thirty years. These giant, moist, irresistible muffins are a must when friends come for a weekend visit in the summer.

2½ cups all-purpose flour

2½ teaspoons baking powder

¼ teaspoon salt

½ cup sugar

1 cup buttermilk

2 large eggs, lightly beaten

½ cup (1 stick) unsalted butter, melted

2 teaspoons vanilla extract

2 cups fresh blueberries, washed and stemmed

12 teaspoons sugar for sprinkling on top of muffins

PLACE an oven rack in the center of the oven and preheat to 400°F. Line 12 muffin cups with paper liners or grease well.

In a medium bowl, stir together the flour, baking powder, salt, and sugar. Add the buttermilk, eggs, melted butter, and vanilla all at once and mix only until the dry ingredients are moistened. Carefully fold in the blueberries.

Spoon the batter into the muffin cups and sprinkle each muffin with 1 teaspoon sugar. Bake for 20 to 22 minutes, until well risen and lightly browned and centers are firm when lightly pressed with a finger. The sugar will have formed a cracked crust. Because of moist berries, a toothpick will not test clean. Allow to cool for 10 minutes in the pan before removing to a wire rack.

Makes 12 large muffins

Whole Orange Muffins

Three whole sweet navel oranges plus golden dried apricots go into these muffins making them vitamin C rich and extremely tasty. Raw sugar sprinkled on the batter bakes to a delicate crunchy topping. This is perfect for breakfast but also delicious with a luncheon chicken salad.

3 large navel oranges

2 large eggs

²/₃ cup safflower oil

¹/₂ cup light brown sugar, firmly packed

¹/₂ teaspoon almond extract

1¹/₄ cups whole-wheat flour

1 cup all-purpose flour

1 teaspoon baking powder

¹/₂ teaspoon baking soda

1 teaspoon ground ginger

1 teaspoon ground cinnamon

¹/₂ teaspoon ground cardamom

¹/₂ teaspoon salt

¹/₂ cup finely chopped dried apricots

2 tablespoons poppy seeds

10 teaspoons raw or turbinado sugar

PLACE an oven rack in the center of the oven and preheat to 400° F. Line 10 muffin cups with paper liners.

Zest two of the oranges and chop finely. Set aside.

Remove the peel and the white pith from all three oranges and cut the pulp, with membranes, into quarters. (If not using navel oranges, remove seeds.) Place in the bowl of a food processor fitted with a metal blade and pulse until pureed. Pour into a measuring cup. There should be 1¹/₂ cups. (Add additional orange pulp if less.) Return to the bowl of the processor and add eggs, oil, brown sugar, almond extract, and reserved orange zest. Pulse to combine.

In a medium bowl, stir together the flours, baking powder, baking soda, ginger, cinnamon, cardamom, and salt. Add the orange mixture to the dry ingredients and stir just until moistened. Gently fold in the apricots and poppy seeds. Spoon into the prepared muffin cups, mounding the batter slightly above the rims of the paper liners. Sprinkle each top with 1 teaspoon of the raw sugar. Bake for 15 to 18 minutes until the centers are barely firm when lightly pressed with a finger or a toothpick inserted into the center of a muffin comes out clean. Allow the muffins to cool for 5 minutes before removing from the pan.

Makes 10 muffins

Candied Cranberry-Spiced Muffins

These super-moist muffins are gorgeously marbled with a sweet/tart cranberry filling. They're perfect for Christmas morning.

For the Filling

3 cups fresh or frozen
  cranberries

1 tablespoon finely chopped
  orange zest

1 cup light brown sugar,
  firmly packed

1/4 teaspoon freshly grated
  nutmeg

2 tablespoons water

For the Batter

2 1/2 cups all-purpose flour

1/4 cup light brown sugar,
  firmly packed

1 tablespoon baking powder

1 teaspoon baking soda

1/2 teaspoon salt

1/2 teaspoon cinnamon

1/2 teaspoon freshly grated
  nutmeg

2 eggs, lightly beaten

6 tablespoons (3/4 stick)
  unsalted butter, melted

3/4 cup lowfat or whole milk

Powdered sugar for dusting tops

PLACE a rack in the center of the oven and preheat to 400°F. Line 12 muffin cups with paper liners or butter well.

To make the filling: In a medium-sized heavy saucepan, combine the cranberries, orange zest, sugar, nutmeg, and water. Cook over moderately high heat until the berries are popped and the mixture has thickened and looks glossy, 5 to 7 minutes. Set aside. The mixture can be made 1 day ahead and refrigerated.

To make the muffin batter: Stir together the flour, sugar, baking powder, baking soda, salt, cinnamon, and nutmeg in a medium bowl. In another bowl, whisk together the eggs, melted butter, and milk. Stir into the dry ingredients with a wooden spoon just until the mixture is moistened. Fold in the candied cranberries and any juices, stirring just until the red mixture is evenly distributed. Spoon the batter evenly into the prepared muffin cups, mounding the batter slightly. Bake on the center rack of the oven for 15 to 18 minutes, until the centers feel firm to the touch. Remove from the oven and allow to rest for 10 minutes before removing to a wire rack.

Dust the tops with powdered sugar before serving.

Makes 12 large muffins

Lowfat Applesauce Muffins

Applesauce replaces some of the oil in these honey-sweetened muffins. It gives them just the right texture and is perfectly in balance with the spices and dried fruit.

⅓ cup safflower oil

½ cup honey

1 cup unsweetened applesauce

2 large eggs

2¼ cups whole-wheat flour

2 teaspoons baking powder

1 teaspoon baking soda

½ teaspoon salt

1 tablespoon ground cinnamon

1 teaspoon ground ginger

½ teaspoon ground allspice

1½ cups dried cranberries, dried cherries, or raisins

PLACE an oven rack in the center of the oven and preheat to 400°F. Line 8 muffin cups with paper liners or grease generously.

In a medium bowl, whisk together the oil, honey, applesauce, and eggs. In another bowl, stir together the flour, baking powder, baking soda, salt, cinnamon, ginger, and allspice. Stir in the applesauce mixture with a wooden spoon. Mix just until all the ingredients are combined. Fold in the cranberries.

Spoon the batter into the muffin cups, mounding slightly. Bake for 20 to 22 minutes, until the centers are firm when lightly pressed with a finger or until a toothpick inserted in the center of a muffin comes out clean. Allow to cool for 10 minutes before removing to a wire rack.

Makes 8 large muffins

Chocolate Buttermilk Muffins

Cherries and chocolate for breakfast? Here, chocolate chips and dried cherries stud a rich, fudgy, bittersweet muffin—a sweet treat for breakfast with strawberries and yogurt or just right with a late-afternoon espresso.

3 ounces unsweetened chocolate

6 tablespoons (¾ stick) unsalted butter

½ cup buttermilk

1 large egg

1 teaspoon vanilla extract

¾ cup light brown sugar, firmly packed

1 teaspoon baking soda

1 cup all-purpose flour

⅓ cup unsweetened cocoa powder, preferably Dutch process

2 teaspoons baking powder

⅓ cup semisweet chocolate chips

⅔ cup dried cherries

Powdered sugar for garnish

PLACE an oven rack in the center of the oven and preheat to 400°F. Line 8 muffin cups with paper liners.

In a small saucepan over low heat, melt the chocolate and butter with the buttermilk. Set aside.

In the bowl of a mixer, beat the egg, vanilla, and sugar until light. Dissolve the baking soda in ¼ cup of boiling water and add to the egg mixture, along with the chocolate. Mix until well combined. Add the flour, cocoa, and baking powder and mix just until incorporated. Stir in the chocolate chips and cherries.

Spoon the batter evenly into the muffin cups and fill to the rim. Bake for 15 to 18 minutes, until the centers are firm when lightly pressed with a finger or a toothpick inserted in the center of a muffin comes out clean. Allow the muffins to cool for 10 minutes before removing to a wire rack. Dust the tops heavily with powdered sugar before serving.

Makes 8 muffins

Thanksgiving Morning Muffins

Light, spicy, and lowfat, these pumpkin-colored muffins are just enough to ward off hunger pangs before the Thanksgiving feast. I make them on any chilly fall morning.

2 large eggs

1 large egg white

¾ cup packed light brown sugar

⅓ cup safflower oil

½ cup sweetened or unsweetened applesauce

1½ cups pumpkin puree, canned or fresh

1½ teaspoons ground cinnamon

¾ teaspoon ground ginger

¾ teaspoon ground allspice

¼ teaspoon freshly grated nutmeg

¼ teaspoon ground cloves

½ teaspoon salt

1 tablespoon baking powder

3 cups all-purpose flour

¾ cup dried cranberries or raisins

PLACE an oven rack in the center of the oven and preheat to 400°F. Line 10 muffin cups with paper liners or grease well.

In a large bowl, beat together the eggs, egg white, sugar, oil, applesauce, pumpkin, cinnamon, ginger, allspice, nutmeg, cloves, and salt. With a wooden spoon, gradually add the baking powder and flour and stir until completely incorporated. Add the cranberries and mix just until well distributed.

Spoon the batter into the muffin cups, mounding the tops high. Bake for 35 minutes, until the centers are firm when lightly pressed with a finger, or a toothpick inserted in the center of a muffin comes out clean. Remove from the oven and cool for 10 minutes in the pan before removing to a wire rack.

Makes 10 very large muffins

Chili Corn Bread Muffins

These mellow golden muffins are perfect partners for eggs, salads, or grilled meats. Use the best imported Parmesan you can find, since it greatly impacts the final flavor of the muffin.

1¼ cups all-purpose flour

¾ cup yellow cornmeal

1 cup corn kernels

1 tablespoon sugar

1 tablespoon baking powder

2 teaspoons ground chili powder

½ teaspoon salt

1 teaspoon baking soda

1 cup freshly grated Parmigiano-Reggiano cheese

¾ cup beer

2 large eggs lightly beaten

4 tablespoons (½ stick) unsalted butter, melted

1 jalapeño chili, seeded and minced

PLACE an oven rack in the center of the oven and preheat to 400°F. Line 7 muffin cups with paper liners or grease well.

In a large bowl, stir together the flour, cornmeal, corn, sugar, baking powder, chili powder, salt, baking soda, and cheese. Pour the beer, eggs, butter, and jalapeño into another bowl and whisk together. Stir into the dry ingredients and mix until just moistened but still lumpy.

Fill the muffin cups to the top and bake for 20 minutes, until the centers are firm to the touch and the tops are very lightly browned.

Makes 7 large muffins

Sweet Potato and Black Pepper Biscuits

I *inherited a fondness for sweet potatoes from my great-grandmother, who ate a sweet potato for breakfast everyday. Slide slices of baked ham between these soft, fragrant biscuits, or scoop up scrambled eggs with them. For a colorful light fall supper, serve them with corn chowder and a green salad.*

1¼ pounds sweet potatoes
  or yams

3 tablespoons orange juice

3 tablespoons unsalted butter,
  melted

1½ cups all-purpose flour

1 tablespoon baking powder

½ teaspoon baking soda

1 teaspoon sugar

½ teaspoon salt

⅛ teaspoon ground cloves

⅛ teaspoon coarsely ground
  black pepper

PLACE an oven rack in the center of the oven and preheat to 400°F. Lightly grease a 9- by 9-inch baking pan or a baking sheet.

Place the sweet potatoes on a baking sheet and bake for 1¼ hours, until very soft. Remove from the oven, leaving the oven on. Cool, peel, and mash enough pulp to equal 1 cup. This can be done several hours ahead.

In a medium bowl, stir the sweet potato, orange juice, and butter together until well combined. Add the flour, baking powder, baking soda, sugar, salt, cloves, and pepper and stir until the dry ingredients are moistened. Knead the mixture in the bowl until a soft dough forms. Turn the dough out onto a well-floured surface and knead 10 to 12 times, until smooth. Pat the dough out to a 6-inch circle ½ inch thick. Cut out 8 biscuits with a 2-inch cutter dipped in flour. Gather the scraps, pat out again, and cut 2 more biscuits.

Place the biscuits, barely touching one another, on the prepared pan and bake for 15 to 20 minutes, until the bottoms are lightly browned.

Makes 10 biscuits

Whole-Wheat Biscuits

My mother served baking powder biscuits on Sunday with fried chicken; my grandmother's cook, LuluBell, made them everyday for every meal. I don't ever remember watching very closely as they were made; maybe the process was just too uncomplicated to capture a child's attention. I do remember, however, that the ones made at home were always much better—with a more biscuit-like texture—than ones we had in restaurants. My version of the southern classics are slightly more rustic and, of course, not meant to replace the originals.

1 cup whole-wheat flour

1 cup all-purpose flour

1 tablespoon baking powder

1/2 teaspoon baking soda

1/2 teaspoon salt

1 tablespoon packed light brown sugar

1/4 cup solid vegetable shortening

4 tablespoons (1/2 stick) cold unsalted butter

2/3 cup lowfat buttermilk

PLACE an oven rack in the center of the oven and preheat to 400°F.

In a medium bowl, combine the flours, baking powder, baking soda, salt, and sugar. Cut in the shortening and butter with 2 knives or a pastry blender until the mixture resembles coarse crumbs. Add the buttermilk and stir with a fork just until the dry ingredients are moistened and a soft, sticky dough is formed. Gather the dough into a ball and remove to a floured surface. Knead gently until smooth, 8 to 10 times. Pat the dough out to an 8-inch circle 3/4 inch thick. Cut out 5 biscuits with a 2 1/2-inch biscuit cutter dipped into flour. Gather the scraps, pat out again, and cut 3 more biscuits.

Place the biscuits on an ungreased baking sheet about 1 inch apart and bake for 15 to 18 minutes. The bottoms of the biscuits will be lightly browned, but the tops will remain light. The biscuits will have nearly doubled in height.

Makes 8 biscuits

Buttermilk Ginger Scones

Scones are traditionally made with heavy cream, but I use a lower-fat substitute—buttermilk—instead. These can be ready in little over an hour.

³/₄ cup buttermilk or plain lowfat yogurt

1 large egg

3 cups all-purpose flour

4 teaspoons baking powder

2 teaspoons ground ginger

¹/₂ cup sugar

¹/₂ teaspoon baking soda

¹/₂ teaspoon salt

¹/₂ cup (1 stick) cold unsalted butter

¹/₂ cup finely chopped candied ginger, rinsed

¹/₂ cup currants, soaked for 10 minutes and drained

PLACE an oven rack in the top third of the oven and preheat to 400°F.

In a small bowl, beat the buttermilk and egg together. In a large bowl, stir together the flour, baking powder, ground ginger, sugar, baking soda, and salt. Cut in the butter with a pastry blender or two knives until the mixture has the texture of coarse crumbs. Stir in the candied ginger and currants. Add the buttermilk mixture and blend with a fork just until a soft dough forms.

Turn the dough out onto a lightly floured surface and knead 5 or 6 times, just until the dough holds together. Place on an ungreased baking sheet. Flatten into an 8-inch disc and cut into 8 wedges, separating them slightly. Bake for 20 minutes, until light brown. Remove and wrap in a linen towel for at least 30 minutes before serving.

Makes 8 large scones

Oatmeal Maple Scones

Earthy and sweet, these fragrant scones are just waiting to be slathered with your best fruit jam.

$^3/_4$ cup coarsely chopped pecans

$1^1/_2$ cups all-purpose flour

2 teaspoons baking powder

$^1/_2$ teaspoon baking soda

$^1/_4$ teaspoon salt

6 tablespoons cold unsalted butter, cut into tablespoons

$^3/_4$ cup old-fashioned oats

$^2/_3$ plain whole or lowfat yogurt

$^1/_4$ cup maple syrup

1 teaspoon maple extract

PLACE an oven rack in the center of the oven and preheat to 350°F.

Spread the pecans on an ungreased baking sheet and place in the oven for 10 minutes, until lightly toasted and fragrant. Cool to room temperature. Turn the oven to 400°F. Grease a baking sheet or cover with parchment paper.

In a food processor fitted with a metal blade, pulse together the flour, baking powder, baking soda, and salt. Add the butter and process until the mixture has the texture of coarse crumbs. Pulse in the oats and pecans. In a small bowl, combine the yogurt, maple syrup, and maple extract. Add to the flour mixture and process just to moisten the ingredients.

With a large spoon, place rounded mounds of dough on the baking sheet. Bake for 15 to 18 minutes, until lightly browned. Cool completely before serving.

Makes 10 large scones

Very Ginger Gingerbread

I love to pair a small square of gingerbread with a wedge of fresh pineapple in the morning. The assertive flavor is both invigorating and soothingly familiar.

½ cup (1 stick) unsalted butter

½ cup packed dark brown sugar

2 large eggs

3 tablespoons minced gingerroot

1 cup dark molasses

1½ teaspoons baking soda

2 cups all-purpose flour

⅓ cup whole-wheat flour

1 teaspoon ground cinnamon

¼ teaspoon freshly grated nutmeg

½ teaspoon ground cloves

1 tablespoon ground ginger

¼ teaspoon salt

¼ teaspoon coarsely ground black pepper

PLACE an oven rack in the center of the oven and preheat to 350°F. Butter and flour an 8- or 9-inch square baking pan.

In a large bowl, cream the butter and sugar. Beat in the eggs, gingerroot, and molasses. Dissolve the baking soda in 1 cup of boiling water and set aside. In a small bowl, combine the flours, cinnamon, nutmeg, cloves, ground ginger, salt, and pepper. Add the flour mixture to the butter mixture alternately with the hot baking soda water, beginning and ending with the flour.

Pour the batter into the prepared pan and bake for 50 to 55 minutes, until the center is firm when lightly pressed with a fingertip or a toothpick inserted in the center comes out clean. Allow to rest 10 minutes before slicing. Serve with warm applesauce, Caramelized Apples and Pears (page 116), or piles of softly whipped cream to which 1 teaspoon of finely chopped candied ginger has been added.

Makes one 8-inch square loaf

Whole-Wheat Banana Poppy Seed Bread

U*se the ripest bananas in the bunch for the most flavorful bread. Toast a thick slice of this moist bread and drizzle it with a little honey for breakfast or a midday snack.*

½ cup (1 stick) unsalted
    butter

¼ cup sugar

½ cup honey

2 large eggs

1½ cups mashed very ripe
    bananas (about 3 medium)

1½ cups whole-wheat flour

½ teaspoon salt

1 teaspoon baking soda

1 tablespoon poppy seeds

P‌LACE an oven rack in the center of the oven and preheat to 350°F. Butter a loaf pan measuring 8" × 4" × 2½".

In a large bowl, cream the butter with the sugar and honey. Beat in the eggs and bananas. In a small bowl, stir together the flour, salt, baking soda, and poppy seeds and add to the butter mixture. Mix just until all the ingredients are well combined. Pour the batter into the prepared pan and bake for 1 hour, until a toothpick inserted in the center of the loaf tests clean. Allow to cool in the pan for 10 minutes, then carefully turn out onto a rack to cool completely.

Makes 1 loaf

Tea and Fruit Bread

Dried figs are plumped overnight in Ceylon tea, giving this bread an exotic flavor. If you do not have loose tea, steep three tea bags in the boiling water.

1 tablespoon black tea leaves

6 ounces dried Black Mission figs (about 14), stems removed

1 cup packed dark brown sugar

2 large eggs

½ cup safflower oil

1½ cups all-purpose flour

1 teaspoon ground cinnamon

1 teaspoon baking soda

½ teaspoon ground cloves

¼ teaspoon freshly grated nutmeg

¼ teaspoon aniseed

In a small heatproof bowl, pour 1 cup of boiling water over the tea and allow to steep for 10 minutes. Place the figs in a small nonreactive bowl and pour the tea through a strainer over the figs. Allow to come to room temperature, then cover with plastic wrap and marinate several hours at room temperature or overnight.

Place an oven rack in the center of the oven and preheat to 350°F. Butter a loaf pan measuring 8" × 4" × 2½".

In a large bowl, beat the sugar and eggs until lightened. Beat in the oil and the fig mixture. Add the flour, cinnamon, baking soda, cloves, nutmeg, and aniseed and mix just until combined. Pour into the pan and bake for 40 to 45 minutes, until a toothpick tests clean when inserted in the center of the loaf. Allow to rest for 5 minutes, then turn out onto a rack to cool completely. The center may sink as the bread cools.

Makes 1 loaf

Baked Applesauce Doughnuts

During my freshman year in college, I gained 10 pounds by eating irresistible, warm, fried doughnuts daily between classes. Brushed lightly with melted butter and baked, these have the irresistible flavor and aroma of fried doughnuts but far less fat. To shape the doughnuts, use a cutter with a removable center piece; it can double as a biscuit/scone cutter. Of course, these can be fried.

1 large egg

²/₃ cup sugar

2 tablespoons safflower oil

¹/₂ cup buttermilk

¹/₂ cup unsweetened
  applesauce

3¹/₄ cups all-purpose flour

¹/₂ teaspoon salt

1 tablespoon baking powder

1 teaspoon baking soda

¹/₂ teaspoon freshly grated
  nutmeg

2 teaspoons ground cinnamon

For the Topping

3 tablespoons unsalted butter,
  melted

¹/₂ cup sugar mixed with ¹/₂
  teaspoon ground cinnamon

IN a large bowl, whisk together the egg, sugar, oil, buttermilk, and applesauce. In a small bowl, stir together the flour, salt, baking powder, baking soda, nutmeg, and cinnamon. Add the flour mixture to the egg mixture and blend. Form into a ball and knead lightly on a floured surface until a soft dough forms. Wrap in plastic wrap and refrigerate for several hours or overnight.

Place an oven rack in the center of the oven and preheat to 400°F. Line a baking sheet with parchment paper or grease well.

Roll out the chilled dough (it will still be soft and slightly sticky) into a ³/₄-inch-thick circle on a well-floured surface. Flouring a doughnut cutter before each cut, cut out 12 doughnuts and "holes," rerolling the scraps when necessary. Place on the prepared baking sheet and bake for 20 to 25 minutes, until the bottoms are lightly browned. While still warm, brush the tops and sides with the melted butter and dip into the cinnamon-sugar mixture.

Makes 12 doughnuts and 12 "holes"

Fruit All Day

I am fortunate to live in California, where the variety of fresh, locally grown fruit is endless. Of course, the best-tasting fruits are those that are just picked, but there are plenty of fruits that are not native to California that I can't imagine going without. For instance, the best berries, to my mind, come from Oregon, Maine, and Arkansas, and the best sour cherries are harvested in Michigan. When they show up in the market, I can't resist the opportunity to use them. ✳ Be choosy when buying fruit. Whenever possible, buy organic. Even though it may not look grocery-shelf perfect, it always tastes better. Ripe fruit not only should be bruise-free but should have a tantalizing fragrance. If you buy it underripe, the fruit will never develop the natural sugars that give sweetness and juiciness to the flesh. ✳ The key to preparing all the recipes in this chapter is choosing seasonal fruits. Use the recipes as guides rather than strict formulas. Better yet, rather than shopping with a specific recipe in mind, go to the market and buy whatever looks fresh and is in season. Be flexible. You might not have anticipated using apricots, but if they are irresistibly golden and soft, buy them and then select a recipe. I make Broiled Fruit (page 115) a lot simply because I can pick whatever fruit is in season and brush it with the sweet, tangy sauce. Among my favorite fruits are figs, and I'm lucky enough to have a grower living down the road who supplies me with several dozen varieties of luscious fresh figs.

When they're in season, I make Fresh Figs in Sweet Vanilla Syrup (page 119) and Pan-Seared Figs with Mascarpone (page 119). When melons are in season, I love to combine the different varieties to make Chilled Melon Chunks in Sweet Watermelon Syrup (page 116). ✳ Whatever fruits you choose—sun-warmed peaches, chubby boysenberries, juicy melons, or creamy bananas—enjoy them on their own throughout the day or sauté, puree, broil, poach, or marinate them to reveal another dimension.

Broiled Fruit

Brushed with a pungent sweet sauce, *fruits passed under the broiler become intensely flavored, glistening jewels. The only fruit that doesn't work here is bananas.*

¼ cup honey

1 tablespoon dark brown sugar

1 tablespoon safflower oil

2 tablespoons orange juice

2 tablespoons balsamic vinegar

2 teaspoons chopped fresh mint

Assorted fresh fruit, such as halved figs; halved and pitted unpeeled apricots; quartered and pitted unpeeled nectarines, peaches, or plums; peeled wedges of papaya, pineapple, or mango

Several sprigs of mint for garnish

PLACE an oven rack 3 inches from the broiler unit and preheat the broiler.

In a small saucepan, stir together the honey, sugar, oil, orange juice, vinegar, and mint. Heat just enough to dissolve the honey, then set aside.

Arrange the fruit, cut sides up, in a shallow baking pan. Brush liberally with the basting sauce and broil just until the edges of the fruit are singed. Arrange on a serving platter and serve warm or at room temperature. Garnish with sprigs of mint.

Makes about ½ cup of basting sauce

Caramelized Apples and Pears

Spoon this instead of maple syrup over whole-wheat pancakes, or top with a big spoonful of plain yogurt.

4 tablespoons unsalted butter

1/2 cup sugar

2 large tart apples, peeled, cored, and cut into 1/2-inch slices

2 slightly underripe pears, peeled, cored, and cut into 1/2-inch slices

1/4 cup apple juice

Freshly grated nutmeg

IN a 10-inch skillet over medium heat, melt the butter, then stir in the sugar. Cook, stirring, until the syrup turns a light caramel brown. Add the apple and pear slices and cook, turning the slices until they are well coated with caramel and beginning to exude juices. Thin juices will dissolve any caramel that may have solidified. Continue cooking for approximately 10 minutes, until the fruit is tender and the liquid has evaporated. The fruit should look glossy and translucent. Stir in the apple juice, sprinkle with nutmeg, and remove from the heat. Cool. Use as a filling for omelets or crêpes or as a topping for pancakes or waffles. This can be refrigerated for up to 1 week.

Makes 2 cups

Chilled Melon Chunks in Sweet Watermelon Syrup

Thirst-quenching melons drenched in a syrup of pureed watermelon are the perfect cool-down on a hot summer day. The syrup can be made two days in advance, but assemble this dish just a few hours before serving.

1/4 cup sugar

1 tablespoon lime juice

2 tablespoons coarsely chopped fresh mint

1 jalapeño chili, seeded and minced

1 pound watermelon, seeded and rind removed

6 cups assorted melon chunks (cantaloupe, honeydew, casaba, Persian, watermelon)

Several mint sprigs for garnish

In a small saucepan, combine the sugar, lime juice, mint, and jalapeño with $\frac{1}{4}$ cup water and bring to a boil. Cover, remove from the heat, and allow to steep for 30 minutes. Meanwhile, puree the watermelon in a blender or food processor. Strain $\frac{1}{4}$ cup of the steeped sugar mixture into the watermelon puree and discard the remainder.

In a large bowl, combine the melon chunks with the syrup and refrigerate for 1 hour. Garnish with mint sprigs and serve.

Serves 4

Broiled Peppered Oranges

Big, easy-to-peel, seedless navel oranges are abundant in the winter when not too many other fruits are. Sliced into thick discs and sprinkled with a sweet/hot mixture, they add pizzazz and color to any plate.

4 navel oranges, peeled and
cut crosswise into 1-inch
discs

$\frac{1}{2}$ cup sugar

$\frac{1}{2}$ teaspoon cinnamon

$\frac{1}{2}$ teaspoon dried crushed red
pepper

Place an oven rack 3 inches under the broiler and preheat the broiler.

Place the orange slices on a baking sheet. In a small bowl, stir together the sugar, cinnamon, and red pepper. Sprinkle approximately $\frac{1}{2}$ teaspoon of the mixture evenly on top of each orange slice. Place under the broiler and cook for 5 to 7 minutes just until the edges are singed and the sugar is bubbling. Remove from the pan with a spatula to a serving plate. Serve warm.

This can accompany grilled chicken, swordfish, or roast duck, as well as pancakes and waffles.

Serves 4

Sautéed Pineapple and Plantain
in Coconut Syrup

If you're in the mood for tropical flavors, serve this as a side dish or on top of a stack of yogurt pancakes. Plantains have nearly black skins when they are ripe and are firmer and drier than bananas, making them great for cooking. If you can't find them, substitute bananas that still have some green at their tips. Buy coconut milk in the Asian food sections of most supermarkets.

1 plantain (approximately ½ pound), peeled and cut on the diagonal into ¼-inch slices

½ fresh pineapple, peeled, cored, and cut into ½-inch wedges

1 cup coconut milk

¼ cup packed dark brown sugar

2 tablespoons unsalted butter

Freshly grated nutmeg

In a 12-inch nonstick skillet over medium-high heat, spread the plantain slices in a single layer and sear on both sides until golden brown, being careful not to scorch. Remove to a platter. Add the pineapple pieces to the skillet and brown on both sides. Remove from the pan and add to the plantain.

In a small bowl, stir the coconut milk and brown sugar together and pour into the hot skillet. Allow the mixture to boil, stirring constantly, until the volume is reduced by half. Add the butter and stir until the mixture becomes a thickened syrup, about 3 minutes. Return the fruit to the skillet and stir to coat with the syrup. Sprinkle with nutmeg and serve.

Serves 4

Fresh Figs in Sweet Vanilla Syrup

Nothing compares to biting through the warm, barely resistant skin of a just-picked fig and coming upon the succulent, seedy flesh. I use the intensely sweet Black Mission figs, but use whatever variety is available and perfectly ripe. If fresh figs are not in season, substitute just over a half pound of dried and simmer 30 minutes after adding the figs. Top with a spoonful of crème fraîche for a yummy dessert.

1½ cups white grape juice

½ cup sugar

1 tablespoon lemon juice

1 moist vanilla bean, split and scraped

20 fresh Black Mission figs or other variety, stems removed (about 1 pound)

IN a medium saucepan over medium heat, stir together the grape juice, sugar, lemon juice, and vanilla bean. Simmer for 5 minutes. Add the figs and cook over low heat for about 15 minutes, until the syrup darkens and the figs are soft. Serve warm over French toast or chilled as a dessert with a dollop of crème fraîche. This can be covered and refrigerated for 2 weeks.

Serves 4

Pan-Seared Figs with Mascarpone

A ripe fig should give easily to gentle pressure and can vary in color from pale green to brown to purplish black. The inside colors vary as well, from pale green to deep red. By barely searing figs, their sweet juices quickly caramelize to intensify their luscious flavor. Serve with cool, delicately flavored mascarpone and a piece of toasted Walnut Bread (page 87).

8 large ripe figs, halved

½ cup mascarpone cheese

¼ cup honey

HEAT a heavy 10-inch skillet over high heat and place the figs in it, cut sides down. Cook just until browned and juices begin to appear. Remove with a spatula to plates, cut sides up. Serve with a dollop of mascarpone and drizzle with honey.

Serves 4

Dried Fruit Poached in Spiced Orange Syrup

Serve these sweet, chewy fruits warm over hot cereal or cold stirred into a cup of vanilla yogurt. Use pears, apples, or giant golden raisins if you like.

2½ cups orange juice

2 cinnamon sticks

1 teaspoon ground cinnamon

¼ teaspoon freshly grated nutmeg

⅛ teaspoon ground cloves

1 cup dried apricots

1 cup dried pitted prunes

1 cup dried peaches

½ cup dried cranberries

¼ cup raisins

IN a medium saucepan, combine the orange juice, cinnamon sticks, ground cinnamon, nutmeg, and cloves and bring to a boil. Add the apricots, prunes, peaches, cranberries, and raisins and stir. Reduce the heat to low and cook for about 30 minutes, until nearly all the liquid has been absorbed. The fruits should look plumped and tender but not breaking apart. They will continue to absorb the syrup as they cool. Remove from the heat and allow to cool to room temperature before storing in the refrigerator. Remove the cinnamon sticks before storing.

Makes about 3 cups

Apple Cider Sauce

Winter mornings were made for this warm homemade applesauce. Start with the most fragrant, flavorful apples, but not necessarily the most tart, since the amount of sugar can easily be adjusted. Make a batch on the weekend to serve warm with a little cinnamon and cream or chilled during the week.

3 pounds firm, fragrant apples, peeled, cored, and each cut into 8 wedges

1 cup unsweetened cider or apple juice

1 moist vanilla bean, split and scraped

½ to ¾ cup packed light brown sugar

PLACE the apples in a large saucepan with the cider and vanilla bean. Bring to a boil, reduce the heat, and simmer for 30 to 40 minutes, until the apples are very soft. Puree in batches in a food processor or blender and return to the pan. Add the sugar to taste and stir over low heat until dissolved. Taste and add more sugar if necessary. The applesauce can be stored, covered, in the refrigerator for up to 1 week.

Makes 6 cups

Breakfast Desserts

It's curious to me that there are endless recipes for desserts to accompany an appropriate lunch or dinner menu and yet never a suggestion for breakfast. I, for one, often feel the compulsion to have just a sliver of pie in the morning or a spoonful of leftover bread pudding. And why do you think coffee bars stock massive quantities of chocolate and other sweet things? It reassures me that I'm not alone in my desire for a real after-meal indulgence at breakfast. As part of a grand buffet for brunch, the dessert cart is a fitting addition, but I have offered a list from which to choose even for lesser occasions. As you begin to enjoy having breakfast all day, don't forget dessert.

Cappuccino Nonfat Breakfast Brownie

Although I call this a breakfast brownie, chocolate lovers know that there's no time like the present to eat chocolate. Cocoa and espresso powder combined with applesauce is the secret to this fat-free, fudgy brownie.

1½ cups whole-wheat flour

¾ cup all-purpose flour

1 cup packed dark brown sugar

1 teaspoon baking powder

½ teaspoon baking soda

3 tablespoons instant espresso powder

⅓ cup unsweetened cocoa powder

1 cup nonfat milk or buttermilk

1 cup unsweetened applesauce

2 teaspoons vanilla extract

½ cup chocolate chips (optional)

PLACE an oven rack in the center of the oven and preheat to 375°F. Generously oil an 8- by 8-inch baking pan.

In a medium bowl, combine the flours, brown sugar, baking powder, baking soda, espresso powder, and cocoa. In another bowl, stir the milk, applesauce, and vanilla together. Stir into the dry ingredients along with the chocolate chips, if using, until a thick batter is formed. Pour into the prepared pan. Bake for 35 minutes, until a toothpick inserted into the center comes out clean. Cool completely before cutting into squares.

Makes 12

Cinnamon Toast Apple Cobbler

New Englanders have been eating cobblers and pies for breakfast for centuries. Make this for dessert tonight, and breakfast will be ready and waiting in the morning (if there's any left ...).

10 slices of cinnamon raisin bread, approximately 3½" × 3½"

4 tablespoons (½ stick) unsalted butter, melted

4 large tart apples (about 1½ pounds), peeled and cut into ¼-inch slices

¾ cup loosely packed light brown sugar

1 teaspoon ground cinnamon

1 tablespoon lemon juice

1 cup unsweetened apple juice

PLACE an oven rack in the lower third of the oven and preheat to 350°F.

Brush one side of each bread slice with the butter and cut into 1-inch squares. Spread out on a rimmed baking sheet and toast for 15 to 20 minutes, until lightly browned. Set aside and leave the oven on.

Meanwhile, in an 8- by 8-inch or 9- by 9-inch baking pan, stir the apple slices with the brown sugar, cinnamon, and lemon juice. Add the toast squares and toss together. Gently pour the apple juice down the sides of the pan around the apple mixture. Cover the pan tightly with foil and bake for 30 minutes. Uncover and stir the cobbler, bringing the bottom and any liquid over the top. Continue baking another 35 to 45 minutes, stirring once, until almost all the liquid has evaporated. Remove from the oven and serve warm or at room temperature with a spoonful of plain lowfat yogurt or crème fraîche.

Serves 6

Pecan Crunch Nectarine Cobbler

Ready to eat in less than an hour, this mouthwatering combination of soft, juicy nectarines and toasty pecans is delicious on its own or dressed with a dollop of whipped cream or scoop of real vanilla ice cream. Best of all, there's no peeling of the fruit.

8 medium ripe nectarines
   (about 2 pounds), pitted
   and each cut into 6 wedges

1/4 cup sugar

1 tablespoon all-purpose flour

1 tablespoon lemon juice

For the Topping

1 cup all-purpose flour

3/4 cup firmly packed light
   brown sugar

1 teaspoon ground cinnamon

1/2 cup (1 stick) unsalted
   butter, cut in 1/2-inch pieces

1/2 cup coarsely chopped
   pecans, lightly toasted

PLACE an oven rack in the center of the oven and preheat to 375°F.

In an 8- by 8-inch baking pan, toss the nectarines with the sugar, flour, and lemon juice.

To make the topping: In a food processor fitted with the metal blade, combine the flour, brown sugar, and cinnamon. Add the butter and process until coarse crumbs are formed. Add the nuts and pulse just until incorporated. Crumble the mixture evenly over the nectarines.

Bake the cobbler for 50 to 55 minutes, until the topping is lightly browned and juices are bubbling around the edges. Remove from the oven and cool 15 minutes before serving. Top with vanilla ice cream or softly whipped heavy cream, if desired.

Serves 6

Orange Risotto Pudding Cake

Arborio rice contains extra starch, which gives risottos their signature creaminess. It does the same here, yet this brunch or breakfast "cake" is firm enough to be cut into wedges. Topped with fresh fruit, it easily becomes a company dessert. It can be made a day in advance.

1 cup arborio rice

4 cups lowfat or whole milk

Pinch of salt

2 cinnamon sticks

5 teaspoons finely chopped
   orange zest

$^2/_3$ cup sugar

$^1/_4$ cup fresh orange juice

1 teaspoon vanilla extract

3 large eggs, at room
   temperature

Powdered sugar for dusting

For the Topping

4 cups fresh strawberries,
   hulled and sliced

$^1/_4$ cup sugar, or to taste

1 tablespoon Grand Marnier
   (optional)

In a medium saucepan, stir together the rice, milk, salt, cinnamon sticks, orange zest, and $^1/_3$ cup of the sugar. Bring to a simmer over medium heat, stirring to prevent the rice from sticking to the bottom of the pan. Reduce the heat to low and continue cooking, stirring regularly, for 15 to 20 minutes, until most of the milk is absorbed and the mixture has a pudding-like consistency. Stir in the orange juice and vanilla. Set aside to cool for at least 1 hour. Remove the cinnamon sticks.

Place an oven rack in the center of the oven and preheat to 350°F. Generously butter and flour a 9-inch springform pan.

In a large bowl, whisk the eggs and remaining $^1/_3$ cup sugar until thick and lemon-colored, about 3 minutes. Add a little of the egg mixture to the rice to lighten it, then fold the rice into the egg mixture until well combined. Pour the mixture into the prepared pan and bake for 40 to 45 minutes, just until the center is set. Remove to a rack to cool. Remove the sides of the pan and sprinkle the top lightly with powdered sugar. Serve the cake immediately or wrap in plastic wrap and refrigerate overnight. Dust with powdered sugar again just before serving.

To make the topping: Toss the strawberries with the sugar and Grand Marnier, if using. Allow to macerate for 30 minutes. Cut the cake into wedges and spoon the strawberries and some of their juices over each piece.

Serves 8

Ricotta Bread Pudding

Although bread puddings have long been thought of as desserts, they are really created from traditional breakfast ingredients —eggs, bread, and cheese. This recipe makes enough to serve warm for dessert and a cold midnight snack or breakfast.

8 slices of French bread, crusts removed and reserved, cut into 1-inch cubes (4 cups)

1½ cups lowfat milk

1 tablespoon Cognac or brandy

½ cup currants

2 large eggs

½ cup sugar

½ teaspoon ground cinnamon

1 teaspoon vanilla extract

¼ teaspoon freshly grated nutmeg

2 teaspoons finely chopped orange zest

5 ounces (⅔ cup) lowfat ricotta cheese

For the Topping

Reserved crusts from French bread

2 tablespoons unsalted butter, melted

¼ teaspoon ground cinnamon

1 tablespoon sugar

PLACE an oven rack in the center of the oven and preheat to 350°F. Butter a 1½-quart soufflé dish.

Place the bread cubes, milk, and Cognac in the soufflé dish and allow to soak for 20 minutes, turning often. Plump the currants in hot water and drain. In a medium bowl, whisk together the currants, eggs, sugar, cinnamon, vanilla, nutmeg, orange zest, and ricotta. Combine with the bread cubes.

To make the topping: In a food processor, grind the crusts to make 1½ cups of crumbs. In a small bowl, combine the crumbs, butter, cinnamon, and sugar.

Top the pudding with the crumb mixture and bake for 35 to 40 minutes, until puffy and lightly browned. Serve warm or chilled.

Serves 6

Persimmon Soufflé Pudding

The large, acorn-shaped Hachiya variety of persimmon with its deep red-orange soft flesh makes a soft, sweet pudding for a fall brunch. It's good warm or chilled topped with plain yogurt or whipped cream.

3 large eggs

¼ cup sugar

2 cups all-purpose flour

1 teaspoon baking soda

1 teaspoon baking powder

½ teaspoon salt

1 teaspoon ground ginger

1 teaspoon cinnamon

1 teaspoon ground coriander

2 cups persimmon pulp (from 4 to 5 persimmons)

1½ cups whole or lowfat milk

3 tablespoons unsalted butter, melted

½ cup golden raisins

PLACE a rack in the center of the oven and preheat to 350°F. Butter an 8- by 8-inch or 9-by 9-inch baking pan.

In a large mixing bowl, beat the eggs and sugar until light and lemon colored. In a medium bowl, stir together the flour, baking soda, baking powder, salt, ginger, cinnamon, and coriander. Place the persimmon pulp in the bowl of a food processor and puree. Pulse in the milk and butter. With the mixer on low speed, add the flour mixture and persimmon puree alternately to the eggs and sugar, beginning and ending with the flour. Stir in the raisins. Pour into the prepared pan and bake for 1 hour. The edges of the pudding will be a rich brown color and will begin to pull away from the sides of the pan. The pudding will sink slightly in the center as it cools.

Cool for 10 minutes before serving or cool to room temperature and chill for several hours or overnight.

Serves 8 to 10

Chilled Summer Berry Pudding

*P*ure, *light, and intensely colored, this easy dessert is nothing more than bread bathed in sweet juices sandwiching delicious berries. To help hold its shape while it chills, place a 2-pound weight on top. It will also make slicing easier. Garnish with a few fresh berries and a dusting of powdered sugar.*

1 cup fresh raspberries

2 cups fresh strawberries, hulled and sliced in half if very large

3 cups fresh blueberries, washed and stemmed

$3/4$ cup sugar

1 tablespoon finely chopped orange zest

1 tablespoon orange juice

1 teaspoon cornstarch

$1/4$ cup Grand Marnier or other orange-flavored liqueur

7 to 10 slices of firm-textured white bread (not sourdough), crusts removed

*T*oss all the berries with the sugar in a medium saucepan. Allow to macerate for 1 hour at room temperature. Add the orange zest and juice to the berries, bring to a boil over medium-high heat, and cook for 5 minutes. Dissolve the cornstarch in the Grand Marnier and stir into the fruit mixture. As soon as the juices have thickened slightly, remove the pan from the heat.

Spoon one quarter of the berries and their juices to evenly cover the bottom of a 9" × 4" × 3" loaf pan or ceramic terrine. Trim the bread to fit tightly into the bottom over the berries and press on it to absorb the juices. Spoon one third of the remaining berries and juices over this layer of bread and press firmly. Add another layer of bread, making sure there are no gaps, and cover with half of the remaining berries. Add the last layer of bread, pressing firmly, and spoon the remaining berries and juices over the bread and down the sides of the pan. Cover tightly with plastic wrap and place the pan on a plate. Weight the pudding evenly with about 2 pounds by placing soup cans or a brick on top. Refrigerate overnight or as long as 2 days.

When ready to serve, run a knife around the inside edge of the pan to loosen the pudding and turn it out onto a serving platter. Serve with whipped cream or crème fraîche. Garnish with extra berries and powdered sugar sprinkled on top.

Serves 6 to 8

Berry-Bottom Brunch Cake

Nutmeg is nice, but mace, the pungent coat of the nutmeg seed, is even better in this summery dessert. Serve this instead of the predictable coffee cake for brunch. Use a combination of blueberries or raspberries if you wish.

For the Topping

2 tablespoons sugar

1/8 teaspoon ground mace

1 tablespoon unsalted butter, softened

For the Berry Mixture

2 cups fresh boysenberries

1/2 cup sugar, or to taste

1 tablespoon all-purpose flour

1/8 teaspoon ground mace

2 tablespoons unsalted butter

For the Cake

1 1/3 cups all-purpose flour

1 teaspoon baking powder

1 teaspoon baking soda

1/4 teaspoon ground mace

Pinch of salt

6 tablespoons unsalted butter, at room temperature

1/2 cup sugar

2 large eggs, at room temperature

1 teaspoon vanilla extract

2/3 cup plain lowfat yogurt

PLACE an oven rack in the center of the oven and preheat to 350°F. Butter a 2-quart baking or soufflé dish.

To make the topping: Mash the sugar, mace, and butter together with a fork in a small bowl. Set aside.

To make the berry mixture: Stir together the berries, sugar, flour, mace, and butter in a medium bowl. Pour into the prepared baking dish.

To make the cake: Combine the flour, baking powder, baking soda, mace, and salt in a small bowl. In a large bowl, cream the butter and sugar until light and fluffy. Beat in the eggs, vanilla, and yogurt. Add the dry ingredients and mix until just incorporated.

Pour the batter over the berries and crumble the topping over the batter. Bake for 50 to 60 minutes, until the top is golden brown. Remove from the oven and cool on a rack for 30 minutes before serving. This can be made several hours ahead and served at room temperature.

Serves 6 to 8

Plum Kuchen

Kuchens are simple, rustic "cakes" that can be served for breakfast as a coffee cake or with whipped cream for dessert. Substitute quartered unpeeled peaches or nectarines or halved apricots for the plums.

1 cup all-purpose flour

½ cup sugar

1 teaspoon baking powder

¼ teaspoon salt

2 large eggs, lightly beaten

1 teaspoon vanilla extract

⅓ cup lowfat or whole milk

¼ cup (½ stick) unsalted butter, melted

5 medium firm-ripe plums (about 1 pound), pitted and quartered

½ teaspoon ground cinnamon mixed with 3 tablespoons sugar for topping

Powdered sugar for dusting

PLACE an oven rack in the lower third of the oven and preheat to 400°F. Butter an 8-inch springform pan.

In a medium bowl, stir together the flour, sugar, baking powder, and salt. Make a well in the center and add the eggs, vanilla, milk, and butter. Stir just until well combined. Spread the batter evenly in the prepared pan.

Place the plums, cut sides down, on top of the batter in concentric circles. Sprinkle with the cinnamon-sugar mixture and bake for 35 to 40 minutes, until the top is lightly browned and nearly covering the plums. Remove from the oven and allow to cool for 10 minutes before removing the sides of the pan. Dust with powdered sugar and serve warm or at room temperature.

Serves 6

Apple and Stilton Tart

Leftover apple pie with a hunk of sharp Cheddar was one of my favorite breakfasts growing up. Then, it probably had more to do with what I thought was getting away with something. Now, I make this simple version with puff pastry expressly for breakfast. Of course, it can be eaten any time of day. Ask your local favorite bakery to sell you their puff pastry—usually made with real butter. The packaged variety in supermarkets is made with oil. Use the best-quality cheese too, since the tart has so few ingredients.

½ pound puff pastry

3 Golden Delicious apples, peeled, cored, and cut into ¼-inch slices

2 tablespoons flour

2 tablespoons sugar

4 ounces English Stilton, Cheshire, or extra-sharp white Cheddar cheese

PLACE an oven rack in the lower third of the oven and preheat to 400°F. Butter a 9-inch tart pan with removable bottom.

On a lightly floured surface, roll the puff pastry to a 13-inch circle ⅛ inch thick. Carefully fit into the tart pan and fold over the edges. Refrigerate for 30 minutes.

Arrange the apple slices in concentric circles, slightly overlapping, on the pastry. In a small bowl, mash the flour, sugar, and cheese together and crumble over the apples. Place on a baking sheet and bake the tart for 45 to 50 minutes, until the edges of the pastry are well browned and the cheese is bubbling. Remove from the oven and cool for 15 minutes before serving. Remove the rim of the pan and cut into wedges.

Serves 6

Strawberry and Buttermilk Tart from the Farm

In searching out inspiration in older, out-of-print cookbooks, I keep stumbling across recipes for buttermilk pie. Here is my version. In days when butter was churned from milk or cream at home, buttermilk was the acidulous by-product. Now sweet, fresh buttermilk is made commercially and gives this silky custard tart a subtle tanginess. Patch any cracks or holes in the pastry to prevent the filling from leaking out. Substitute seasonal fruits such as peaches, nectarines, blueberries, or even mangoes for the strawberries.

For the Pastry

One ¼-ounce package dry yeast

⅓ cup warm water (105° to 110°F.)

2 cups all-purpose flour

½ teaspoon salt

¾ cup (1½ sticks) cold unsalted butter, cut into tablespoon-sized pieces

2 large egg yolks

For the Filling

3 large eggs, at room temperature

¾ cup sugar

2 cups buttermilk

½ teaspoon finely chopped lime zest

2 tablespoons fresh lime juice

1 large egg white mixed with 1 teaspoon water for brushing pastry

2 cups fresh strawberries, hulled and thinly sliced lengthwise

Powdered sugar for garnish

To make the pastry: In a small bowl, sprinkle the yeast over the water and allow to dissolve for 5 minutes until foamy. In a food processor or large bowl, combine the flour and salt. Cut in the butter by processing or by hand, using a pastry blender or 2 knives, until the mixture resembles coarse crumbs. Pour in the yeast and yolks and process or mix until the mixture forms a ball. Turn the dough out onto a lightly floured surface and allow to rest, covered with a towel, for 10 minutes. Roll out the dough until ¼ inch thick. Fit into a 9-inch deep-dish pie pan or quiche dish. Fold the excess dough and form a decorative border slightly higher than the rim of the pan. Make sure all the surfaces are smooth and sealed. The filling will come to the top of the dish, and the pastry needs to be thick enough to support it.

Place an oven rack in the lower third of the oven and preheat to 350°F.

To make the filling: In a medium bowl, beat the eggs and sugar until thick, light, and lemon-colored, about 5 minutes. Add the buttermilk, lime zest, and juice and beat until well combined. Carefully pour into the pastry shell. It will be very full. Brush the pastry edge with egg wash and bake for 45 to 50 minutes, until the outside edge of the filling is set but the center still jiggles. Remove from the oven, cool to room temperature, and chill, covered, overnight.

To serve: Arrange the strawberry slices in concentric circles on top of the pie. Sprinkle generously with powdered sugar and serve immediately.

Serves 6

Preserves, Spreads, and Syrups

To my mind, the feature attractions at breakfast are the condiments. Ordinary bread or a plain pancake can be transformed by a drizzle of homemade fruity syrup or a swipe of luscious preserves. By using organically grown local fruit, you can make a lightly sweetened syrup or compote that bears no resemblance to the bottled versions—the quality and taste are beyond compare. By making preserves, fruit toppings, syrups, and spreads in your own kitchen, you can control the amount of sugar and the quality of the fruit and other ingredients. ✳ The beauty of the recipes in this chapter is in the latitude they allow. Make Fruited Maple Syrup (page 142) any time of year with seasonal fruits. If mangoes are in season, use them in place of the bananas in Sweet Orange and Banana Syrup (page 142). You'll never eat plain cream cheese again once you try the smoked salmon Cream Cheese Spread (page 141) or other varieties I share. Whether you're having waffles for breakfast, pancakes for dinner, or a bagel for a snack, there's a condiment here that will make it special.

Blood Orange Marmalade

They may look like regular juice oranges on the outside, but blood oranges bear no resemblance to them on the inside. Slice one open to find dazzling burgundy flesh. The flavor is also somewhat sharper, with overtones of raspberry. Look for blood oranges in gourmet markets or specialty food stores.

2½ pounds blood oranges (9 to 10)

¼ cup regular orange juice

1½ cups sugar

½ cup light corn syrup

⅛ teaspoon finely ground black pepper

Zest all the oranges. There should be ½ cup, packed. Juice enough of the oranges to yield 1 cup of blood orange juice. Peel the remaining oranges and pulse the pulp in a food processor until chopped into small pieces. There should be approximately 3 cups of pulp. Stir the pulp, zest, blood orange juice, regular orange juice, sugar, corn syrup, and pepper together in a large bowl. Cover and refrigerate overnight.

Pour the mixture into a large skillet and place over medium heat. Bring to a boil and cook until the marmalade looks glossy and thick and is reduced by approximately one-third, about 30 minutes. Remove a tablespoonful to a saucer and freeze for 3 minutes. Pull your finger through the marmalade. If it wrinkles together, it is ready to jar. Cook another 5 minutes if it doesn't and re-test.

Makes four 6-ounce jars

Winter Jam

Slather this mix of sweet, juicy pineapples and dried apricots on a thick slice of whole-grain toast for a winter pick-me-up. Make sure you allow the apricots to fully soften in the water so they will puree to a smooth, thick paste.

½ pound dried apricots

1 cup orange juice

½ fresh pineapple (about 1½ pounds), cored, peeled, and cut in 2-inch chunks

1 cup sugar

2 tablespoons lime juice

2 tablespoons honey

In a medium saucepan over medium heat, simmer the apricots in the orange juice and 1 cup of water for 15 to 20 minutes, until very soft. With a slotted spoon, remove the fruit, reserving the liquid in the pan, and puree in a food processor until smooth. Add the pineapple to the processor and pulse until only small pieces of pineapple remain. Pour the mixture back into the saucepan with the liquid and stir in the sugar, lime juice, and honey. Cook over medium heat, stirring occasionally, for 1 hour, until the mixture is very thick and all the liquid has been absorbed. Pour into two 10-ounce jars and refrigerate. This will keep, refrigerated, for several weeks.

Makes 2½ cups

Yogurt Cheese

While the health benefits of yogurt have long been touted, to me its ability to transform itself into a tangy spreadable dip is miraculous. Sweeten and serve with fruit, or puree with finely chopped spinach and green onions for a vegetable dip. It makes a perfect topping for baked potatoes, potato pancakes, and even gingerbread. Unadorned, it is an unbeatable spread on warm bagels or waffles.

> 2 cups plain nonfat, lowfat,
> or plain yogurt, preferably
> without pectin or gelatin

LINE a strainer with a coffee filter and place over a small bowl. Pour in the yogurt and cover strainer and bowl tightly with plastic wrap. Refrigerate for 12 to 48 hours. The longer the yogurt is allowed to drain, the thicker it will become. Scoop into a plastic container, cover, and store for as long as 2 weeks. Season to taste for various uses.

Makes about 1 cup

Low-Calorie Toppings

Pureed fruits, smooth cheeses—even a squeeze of lemon can transform an ordinary bagel or piece of toast.

Peaches, apricots, or plums pureed with a dash of cinnamon in a food processor or blender

*

Warm, unsweetened applesauce sprinkled with freshly grated nutmeg

*

Lowfat cottage cheese blended with soft tofu, goat cheese, or yogurt

*

A spoonful of unsweetened fruit preserves stirred into Yogurt Cheese

*

A squeeze of lemon and powdered sugar sprinkled on pancakes, waffles, and French toast

Cream Cheese Spreads

Sweet and savory mix-ins for an old standby. If you're a purist, slather cream cheese on your bagel and enjoy—but if you're in the mood for something special, it only takes a few simple ingredients.

To 8 ounces cream cheese, add:

2 ounces smoked salmon, cut into small pieces

½ teaspoon horseradish

1 tablespoon finely chopped fresh chives

or

1 teaspoon chopped fresh thyme

1 tablespoon chopped fresh basil

1 tablespoon chopped flat-leaf parsley

1 teaspoon lemon juice

or

½ cup mashed ripe strawberries or raspberries

2 tablespoons sugar

2 teaspoons orange juice

Honey Apple Syrup

Three ingredients are all you need to make this delectable syrup. Make it in between flips of the pancakes.

1 cup mild honey

2 tablespoons unsalted butter

¼ cup unsweetened apple juice, preferably unfiltered

IN a small saucepan over low heat, combine the honey, butter, and apple juice. Cook just until the butter has melted. Remove from the heat and stir until blended.

Makes approximately 1⅓ cups

Fruited Maple Syrup

Pure maple syrup and fresh, ripe fruit
are hard to beat on their own, but when they are combined, the flavor is sublime.

1 cup diced fresh fruit, such as
   peaches, apricots, plums,
   bananas, blueberries,
   strawberries, or a
   combination

1 cup real maple syrup

1 moist vanilla bean, split and
   scraped

IN a food processor or blender, puree 1/2 cup of the fruit.

In a small saucepan over medium heat, bring the maple syrup to a simmer. Add the pureed fruit and vanilla bean, reduce the heat to low, and cook for 10 minutes. Stir in the remaining fruit and cook just to heat through. Remove the vanilla bean. Serve over pancakes, waffles, or French toast.

Makes approximately 2 cups

Sweet Orange and Banana Syrup

Homemade syrup is so simple to make
and allows you to control the amount of sugar you use. Puree your favorite fruit,
add a little sweetener, a pinch of spice, and your topping is ready.

3 juice oranges, peeled, pith
   removed, halved, and seeded

1 large banana, peeled

1/2 cup light corn syrup

1/4 teaspoon ground ginger

Pinch of freshly grated nutmeg

PLACE the oranges and banana in a food processor and puree until only small pieces of fruit are visible. Add the corn syrup, ginger, and nutmeg and pulse until combined. Pour into a small saucepan and heat just to boiling. Reduce the heat and simmer for 10 minutes. Serve warm. Can be stored, covered and refrigerated, for 4 days.

Makes 1 3/4 cups

Pineapple Jalapeño Syrup

Serve this sweet-hot syrup with Thin and Crispy Cornmeal Crêpes (page 29) or a quesadilla. It also makes a great dipping sauce for corn fritters.

½ cup sugar

½ fresh pineapple, peeled, cored, and cut into 1-inch chunks (about 3 cups)

2 jalapeño chilies, seeded and minced

Pinch of cayenne

Pinch of salt

COMBINE ½ cup water and the sugar in a small saucepan and bring to a boil over medium-high heat. Cook for 3 minutes to dissolve the sugar, then set aside. Puree the pineapple in a food processor or blender and stir in the sugar syrup and jalapeños. Season to taste with cayenne and salt. This can be stored in a nonreactive container, covered and refrigerated, for up to 1 week.

Makes 2 cups

Apple Cider Syrup

Run out of maple syrup? Chances are you have all the ingredients in your pantry to make this aromatic syrup.

2 cups apple cider or apple juice

1 cinnamon stick

⅓ cup loosely packed light brown sugar

2 teaspoons cornstarch

1 tablespoon lemon juice

¼ teaspoon ground mace

1 tablespoon unsalted butter

IN a small saucepan over medium-high heat, bring the cider and cinnamon stick to a boil and cook until reduced by half, about 10 minutes. Remove the cinnamon stick and discard. Stir in the brown sugar. Dissolve the cornstarch in the lemon juice and add to the cider. Bring to a boil again and cook, stirring constantly, until slightly thickened. Remove from the heat and stir in the mace and butter. Cool for 10 minutes before serving.

Makes about 1¼ cups

Fresh Blueberry Syrup

Although you can use frozen blueberries, this intensely flavored syrup is best when made from inexpensive midsummer berries. It keeps for several weeks in the refrigerator, waiting to be lavished on warm pancakes or French toast.

2 cups fresh blueberries, washed and stemmed

½ cup unsweetened apple juice

⅓ cup sugar, or to taste

⅓ cup light corn syrup

2 teaspoons lemon juice

STIR the blueberries, apple juice, sugar, corn syrup, and lemon juice together in a medium saucepan. Place over high heat and bring to a boil. Lower the heat to medium and cook, stirring occasionally, for 5 minutes, or until the berries pop. The syrup will be thin. Remove from the heat and cool for 15 to 20 minutes before serving. The syrup will thicken as it cools.

Makes 2 cups

Super Chocolate Syrup

Just a little of this intensely chocolaty syrup gives milk, ice cream, or hot cocoa a deep fudgy flavor. It will keep indefinitely in the refrigerator.

½ cup unsweetened cocoa powder, preferably Dutch process

1 cup packed dark brown sugar

1 teaspoon instant coffee granules

¼ teaspoon ground cinnamon

1 teaspoon vanilla extract

POUR 1 cup of water into a small saucepan and whisk in the cocoa powder, sugar, instant coffee, and cinnamon until dissolved. Bring the mixture just to a boil over medium heat, whisking, then remove from the heat. Stir in the vanilla. Cool to room temperature, then cover and refrigerate.

Makes 1½ cups

_____ Variation _____

To make hot cocoa, stir 1 tablespoon of Super Chocolate Syrup into 6 ounces of hot milk.

❋

It can also be stirred into cold milk for chocolate-flavored milk.

Beverages

When my children were in grammar school, there were plenty of mornings when neither of them wanted breakfast. But they never turned down milk shakes. Whipped up in a matter of seconds, these deceptively nutritious drinkable meals appealed to them and soothed my nerves. Breakfast milk shakes are great places to hide vegetables and fruits that your children wouldn't otherwise eat. The combination possibilities are endless, and by following my instincts, I almost always created something my kids happily drank. ✻ Many of the drinks begin with plain lowfat or nonfat yogurt. Look at the ingredients list on yogurt cartons and choose brands that do not contain gelatin, pectin, or added sugars. The purest and freshest yogurts are often found in kosher or health food markets. To avoid having to add ice cubes, I try to include at least one frozen fruit. A frozen banana adds incredible creaminess and just the right amount of banana flavor. Stock your freezer with bags of frozen fruit without added sugar. Freeze your own fresh fruit by spreading berries or sliced peaches, nectarines, or unpeeled plums on a baking sheet and placing it in the freezer. When solid, pack the fruit in plastic freezer bags. Wrap peeled bananas separately in plastic, then freeze. Keep cans of frozen juice concentrate on hand too. Spoon a little into the blender for a frosty jolt of intense flavor. To keep the creamy texture of an ice cream shake, I add a little nonfat milk powder, which also ups the calcium count without adding fat. I also use dense fresh fruits, like papayas, bananas, mangoes, peaches, nectarines, and apricots in greater quantities than berries, melons, and pineapples. Add a tablespoon or two of vitamin- and mineral-rich protein powder, available at health food stores, to the blender for a nutritionally balanced blender drink. ✳ Don't limit blender drinks to breakfast. If your energy dips in the afternoon, toss together a Chocolate Banana Shake (page 151) or a Strawberry Yogurt Smoothie (page 150). If you crave a light snack, Orange Iced Coffee (page 155) or a Pineapple Papaya Soother (page 150) can take the edge off your hunger until it's time to eat. Whatever the time of day, use your imagination to create your own favorite breakfast, lunch, and dinner shakes.

Almost Orange Julius

I'm sure I'm one of dozens of fans who have tried to re-create the flavor of an authentic Orange Julius. The recipe remains a closely guarded secret, but my interpretation—wholesome, frothy, and easy to make—is definitely reminiscent of the original.

This recipe is simple enough for kids to make for a satisfying after-school thirst quencher. Honey may replace the corn syrup, and other fruit juices may be substituted for the orange juice.

1 cup orange juice

½ cup nonfat dry milk

1 tablespoon light corn syrup

½ teaspoon vanilla extract

2 ice cubes

PLACE all the ingredients in a blender and process on high speed until frothy.

Makes one 10-ounce drink

Carob Protein Punch

*W*hether you're avoiding chocolate or not, try carob powder, which is lower in fat and naturally sweet. Look for it in health food stores and some supermarkets.

1½ cups nonfat milk

½ cup nonfat dry milk

2 tablespoons molasses

1 tablespoon protein powder

2 tablespoons carob powder

2 ice cubes

Pinch of ground cinnamon

PLACE the milk, dry milk, molasses, protein powder, carob, and ice in a blender and process on high speed until well combined. Scrape down the sides of the blender container if necessary and continue blending until smooth. Pour into a tall glass and sprinkle with cinnamon.

Makes one 12-ounce drink

Strawberry Yogurt Smoothie

There are just some mornings when nothing goes according to schedule and you feel rushed and anxious about the day. Smoothies are meant for these times. Wrap a peeled banana in plastic and freeze overnight. The next morning, throw this short list of ingredients into the blender and puree. Pour into an insulated glass or mug and sip the smoothie on your way to work. You'll arrive ready for the day.

1 banana, peeled, cut into 4 pieces, and frozen

6 fresh or frozen strawberries

1 tablespoon honey

1 tablespoon unprocessed bran

2 tablespoons nonfat dry milk (optional)

1 teaspoon vanilla extract

1 cup plain lowfat or nonfat yogurt

PLACE the banana, strawberries, honey, bran, dry milk, if using, vanilla, and yogurt in a blender. Process on high speed until completely smooth. Scrape the sides of the container if necessary and blend again. Pour into a glass. If the mixture is too thick, add a few tablespoons of lowfat milk.

Makes one 16-ounce drink

Pineapple Papaya Soother

Because it is impossible to drink this quickly, the soothing effects of it are lasting and sustaining. There is always flexibility for substitutions in these drinks, so don't hesitate to toss in other fruits: banana chunks, mango slices, strawberries, half a peach, or a couple of pitted apricots.

½ cup frozen orange juice concentrate, undiluted

½ cup plain lowfat yogurt

⅓ cup lowfat milk

2 tablespoons unprocessed bran

¼ cup nonfat dry milk (optional)

½ papaya, peeled, seeded, and cut into chunks

½ cup pineapple chunks

2 teaspoons honey (optional)

WITHOUT thawing the orange juice concentrate, spoon it into a blender with the yogurt, milk, bran, dry milk, if using, papaya, and pineapple. Process on high speed until completely smooth, scraping the sides of the container if necessary. Taste and add the honey, if desired.

Makes one 16-ounce drink

Chocolate Banana Shake

A chocolate-covered banana in a glass. Creamy, sweet frozen yogurt blended with extra protein powder and a banana makes for a highly fortified breakfast.

8 ounces chocolate frozen
  lowfat or nonfat yogurt

$^{1}/_{2}$ banana, peeled and frozen

1 tablespoon protein powder
  (optional)

$^{1}/_{2}$ cup nonfat dry milk

1 teaspoon vanilla extract

PLACE the frozen yogurt, banana, protein powder, if using, dry milk, and vanilla in a blender and process for 1 minute, until completely smooth.

Makes one 12-ounce drink

--- Variation ---

1 single-serving envelope
  sugar-free cocoa mix

❋

$^{1}/_{2}$ cup lowfat milk

❋

$^{1}/_{2}$ banana, peeled and frozen

❋

1 teaspoon vanilla extract

Place the cocoa mix, milk, banana, and vanilla in a blender and process for 1 minute, until completely smooth.

Makes one 10-ounce drink

Mona's Breakfast to Go

My friend Mona is incredibly fit. She's also smart, attractive, strong, and very funny. As I was finishing this book, I asked her what she liked to eat for breakfast. Prepared to listen to a list of heart-healthy foods, I was stunned when she replied, "Potato chips." Yes, for much of her adult life she began (and ended) her day with potato chips. But a few years ago she started drinking this yogurt milk shake and noticed such a difference in her day's energy level that she gave up the potato chip menu for good.

8 ounces plain lowfat or nonfat yogurt	1 fresh mango, peeled and sliced
1 tablespoon unprocessed bran	2 tablespoons honey
¼ cup orange juice	2 ice cubes (optional)

PLACE the yogurt, bran, orange juice, mango, honey, and ice cubes, if using, in a blender and process on high speed until completely combined.

Makes one 20-ounce drink

Hot Spiced Cider

On a wintry afternoon, take a break and enjoy a warming cup of this spiced cider. Try it at breakfast too, to give your insides a glow.

8 cups fresh apple cider	½ cup chopped dried apple slices
¼ teaspoon freshly grated nutmeg	4 cinnamon sticks
½ teaspoon ground ginger	Sprigs of fresh thyme for garnish
½ teaspoon vanilla extract	

IN a medium saucepan, heat the apple cider to a simmer. Stir in the nutmeg, ginger, vanilla, apple pieces, and cinnamon sticks and cook for 10 minutes. Pour into large mugs and garnish with a sprig of thyme.

Serves 6 to 8

Pineapple Ginger Cooler

Juicy pineapple pulp combined with the bite of crystallized ginger makes a tingling and refreshing drink. For cocktails, add an ounce of rum.

1 cup pineapple chunks

½ cup nonfat dry milk

3 ice cubes

2 tablespoons finely chopped crystallized (candied) ginger

PLACE the pineapple, milk, ice cubes, and ginger in a blender and process at high speed until completely smooth and frothy.

Makes one 10-ounce drink

Old-Fashioned Orangeade

Starting with real orange juice, you can make a very refreshing juice spritzer that is reminiscent of orange soda pop, only healthier. Make this for a sparkling brunch drink.

2 cups fresh orange juice

½ cup fresh lemon juice

1 cup sugar

2 teaspoons finely grated orange zest

3 cups soda water or seltzer

4 sprigs of fresh mint for garnish

PLACE the juices, sugar, and zest in a blender and process for 30 seconds. Add the soda water and blend. Pour over ice into 4 glasses and garnish each with a sprig of mint.

Makes four 12-ounce drinks

Pineapple Citrus Drink

Eating a whole orange or grapefruit is a lot more nutritious than just drinking the juice. The fiber rich pulp is full of vitamins. This super refreshing drink offers the best of both.

1 large grapefruit

1 large orange

1 cup unsweetened pineapple
   juice

Sprigs of fresh mint for
   garnish (optional)

REMOVE the peel and white pith from the grapefruit and orange. Slice in half through the middle and remove any seeds. Place in a blender and puree. Add the pineapple juice and blend. Serve over ice or refrigerate until chilled. Stir before serving. Garnish with sprigs of mint, if desired.

Makes two 12-ounce drinks

Peaches and Creamy Tofu Shake

I discovered soft tofu rather late in life. I steered away from something I thought would be too difficult to cook with. But soft tofu is really more versatile than its firmer cousin—and a perfect blender ingredient. If you've never had the inclination to try tofu, this is a good time to discover how chameleon-like it is.

4 ounces soft tofu

2 tablespoons nonfat dry milk

1 tablespoon honey

2 ripe peaches, peeled and
   pitted

1/4 teaspoon almond extract

PLACE the tofu, milk, honey, peaches, and almond extract in a blender and process on high speed until the mixture is completely smooth. Pour into a glass.

Makes one 12-ounce drink

Spiced Mocha Chocolate

Better than the coffee bar's, this is one of my favorite drinks, whether as an afternoon reward or a special treat on a weekday morning.

1 cup lowfat or whole milk

2 cups hot strong brewed coffee

2 tablespoons Super Chocolate Syrup (page 145)

2 tablespoons sugar

1 teaspoon ground cinnamon

HEAT the milk in a small saucepan over medium heat. Start whisking the milk vigorously as it warms and continue until it is steaming but does not come to a boil.

Fill a large mug two thirds full with coffee and stir in the chocolate syrup. In a small bowl, combine the sugar and cinnamon. Add to the coffee mixture to taste and top with the frothy milk.

Serves 2

Orange Iced Coffee

Try this cooling refresher when the temperature is high and your energy is low.

1 cup lowfat milk

Grated zest of 1 orange

1 moist vanilla bean, split and scraped

$^1/_2$ cup firmly packed light brown sugar

$1^1/_2$ cups strong brewed coffee, cooled to room temperature

IN a small saucepan, heat the milk, zest, and vanilla bean over medium heat. Simmer for 5 minutes and remove from the heat. Stir in the sugar and cover the pan. Allow the mixture to steep for $^1/_2$ hour. Stir in the coffee and pour over crushed ice or pour into a blender container with 3 ice cubes and blend.

Makes two 12-ounce drinks

Spiced Tea

When served hot, this wonderfully scented tea fills the room with a festive fragrance. Serve it over ice for a tingling, refreshing treat.

Four ¼-inch slices gingerroot, peeled

1 cinnamon stick

5 whole cloves

3 tablespoons sugar

2 strips orange zest, about 3 inches long

2 sprigs of fresh mint

3 tablespoons leaf tea

Milk (optional)

Sprigs of fresh mint for garnish (optional)

In a medium saucepan, bring 4 cups of water to a boil and add the ginger, cinnamon stick, cloves, sugar, orange zest, and mint. Cover the pan and remove from the heat. Allow to steep for 30 minutes. Add the tea and bring to a boil. Reduce the heat and simmer for 5 minutes. Strain into a large glass container for iced tea or directly into cups if serving hot. Add milk to the hot tea, if desired, and adjust the sugar to taste. If serving iced tea, garnish each glass with a mint sprig, if desired.

Makes 4 cups

Index

pineapple(s):
  braised chicken livers with
    Canadian bacon and,
    49
  broiled fruit, 115
  citrus drink, 154
  ginger cooler, 153
  jalapeño syrup, 143
  papaya soother, 150–151
  and plantain in coconut
    syrup, sautéed, 118
  winter jam, 139
pine nuts, Provençal sweet
    spinach tart with, 17
pipérade:
  as appetizer, 12
  baked eggs on, 12
pizza, thin-crusted, 44
plantain and pineapple in
    coconut syrup, sautéed,
    118
plum(s):
  fruited maple syrup, 142
  kuchen, 132
  poached fruit, 115
polenta, saffron, with
    ratatouille and
    Parmesan, 38
popover pancake, 30
poppy seed(s):
  pancakes, 22
  whole-wheat banana bread,
    109
potato(es):
  and artichoke frittata, 7
  baby, egg salad with
    asparagus and, 72
  and fennel pancakes, 26
  savory zucchini pancakes,
    27
  and spinach stir-fry, herbed,
    40
  tomato galette, 41
  wedges, roasted New
    Mexican, 42–43
prosciutto:
  fresh fig, and Parmesan
    sandwich, 48
  and peas, white beans and
    orecchiette, 71
protein punch, carob, 149
Provençal sweet spinach tart
    with pine nuts, 17
pudding:
  cake, orange risotto, 127

chilled summer berry,
    130
  cranberry cinnamon brown
    rice, 60
  persimmon soufflé, 129
  ricotta bread, 128
pull-apart sugar and spice
    brioche, 78–79
pumpkin muffins, Thanksgiving
    morning, 102
punch, carob protein, 149
pure and simple whole-wheat
    bread, 86

Quick bread:
  tea and fruit, 110
  very ginger gingerbread,
    109
  whole-wheat banana poppy
    seed, 109
quinoa, 63

Raised waffles, Fannie
    Farmer's, 32
raisin and toasted seeds bread,
    89
rarebit, Stilton, and oven-
    roasted tomatoes, 43
ratatouille, saffron polenta
    with Parmesan and, 38
red pepper, eggplant, and
    Parmesan frittata, 9
rice:
  -flour pancakes, 25
  orange risotto pudding cake,
    127
  pudding, cranberry
    cinnamon brown,
    60
ricotta bread pudding, 128
risotto pudding cake, 127
roll(s):
  overnight cinnamon twists,
    83
  smoked salmon, 51
  whole-wheat cinnamon,
    cupcakes, 84–85
  see also biscuits; muffins;
    scones

Saffron polenta with
    ratatouille and
    Parmesan, 38
sage:
  and apple cheese soufflé, 19
  and turkey sausage patties,
    46
salad:
  bacon and egg, 67
  berries and spinach, 70
  breakfast, with French toast
    croutons, 68
  egg, with baby potatoes and
    asparagus, 72
  white beans and orecchiette
    with peas and
    prosciutto, 71
  wild mushroom, walnut, and
    watercress, 66
  wild rice, 69
salmon:
  -burgers, 50–51
  cream cheese spread,
    smoked, 141
  fennel and potato pancakes,
    26
  roll, smoked, 51
sandwich:
  French toast ham, 34
  fresh fig, prosciutto, and
    Parmesan, 48
  honeyed French toast, 34
sauce:
  ancho chili and tomato, for
    poached eggs, 13
  apple cider, 121
  tomatillo, for *huevos
    ranchitos*, 20
sausage:
  patties, sage and turkey, 46
  savory topping, for popover
    pancake, 30
scones:
  buttermilk ginger, 106
  oatmeal maple, 107
scrambled eggs:
  and pan-seared mushrooms
    and peppers, 11
  with pasta, soft, 10
seed(s):
  multi-, multi-grain, multi-
    nut granola, 58
  toasted, and raisin bread, 89
shake(s):
  chocolate banana, 151